JOHN PAUL II

Speaks to Religious

1983–1984

Book III

Dean of the Faculty of Canon Law at the Gregorian University in Rome and Consultor for various Congregations and Commissions of the Roman Curia, Father Jean Beyer, of the Society of Jesus, is also known for his many works on consecrated life.

The present compilation of the talks of the Holy Father follows those which appeared in 1981: **"John Paul II Speaks to Religious, 1978–1980,"** and in 1984: **"John Paul II Speaks to Religious, 1981–1982."**

JOHN PAUL II
SPEAKS TO RELIGIOUS

**Principal Allocutions and Letter
from January 1983 to December 1984**

**Compiled and arranged with a Synopsis
by Father Jean Beyer, S.J.**

DISTRIBUTORS

LITTLE SISTERS OF THE POOR
2325 North Lakewood Avenue
Chicago, Illinois 60614
U.S.A.

Headingley Lane
Leeds L S 6 2 BX
England

Sybil Hill Road
Raheny
Dublin 5
Ireland

Market Street
P.O. Box 246
Randwick, N.S.W. 2031
Australia

INFORMATION CONCERNING
THE SYNOPSIS

The outline and chapter headings (**in Roman numerals**) of the present Synopsis are identical with those found in the Synopses of Book I and Book II.

The Synopsis of this present book (Book III) includes new topics (*printed in italic type*) which correspond to other aspects of religious and sacerdotal life emphasized by John Paul II during the years 1983 and 1984.

Certain topics which appeared in the first or second Synopsis have not been repeated; for this reason the numbering (**Arabic numerals in bold type appearing at the left hand margin**) does not follow exactly the outline of the preceding Synopses.

For each topic, one or several numbers (in regular type) refer the reader to a corresponding paragraph within an Allocution or Letter of this present book.

Information concerning footnotes:
Book I refers to **"John Paul II Speaks to Religious, 1978–1980"** compiled and arranged with a Synopsis by Father Jean Beyer, S.J.

Book II refers to **"John Paul II Speaks to Religious, 1981–1982"** compiled and arranged with a Synopsis by Father Jean Beyer, S.J.

Book III refers to **"John Paul II Speaks to Religious, 1983–1984"** compiled and arranged with a Synopsis by Father Jean Beyer, S.J.

The translations of these texts were taken, for the most part, from the *English Edition of L'Osservatore Romano;* the allocution addressed to the Religious of the Hospitaller Order of Saint John of God (December 23, 1984) was reprinted with permission from *Documents N.5* of the General Curia of the Hospitaller Order of Saint John of God. Revisions and additions were made by translating texts from the *French Edition of L'Osservatore Romano, La Documentation Catholique,* and *Jean-Paul II aux Religieuses et Religieux 1983–1984*—Tome III; certain allocutions and a letter were translated in their entirety from these same sources.

INTRODUCTION

The texts of Pope John Paul II, given as addresses, letters or messages to men and women religious in general, or to members of certain Institutes in particular, during the years 1983-1984, have been compiled in this third book.

The synopsis at the beginning of the book facilitates a more systematic study and a more precise consideration of the texts. It shows that the Pope is constantly deepening the doctrine on consecrated life, and especially that which constitutes the essential of that life, that which makes the religious life better understood and lived as a manifestation of the profundity of all Christian life.

Faithful to the Council in which he participated, Pope John Paul II has desired to present the doctrine of Vatican II from the very beginning of his pontificate, and he continues to present it in all its fullness. He thus supports its renewal, its progress and its influence. His teaching makes us discover new or neglected aspects, all based on the long tradition of the Church and the experiences of Founders and Foundresses. These new or at least complementary aspects help to enlighten and enrich the doctrine set forth during the previous years.

Taking a close look at the synopsis, one will see the new subtitles which have been added to each section.

This synopsis has kept its original structure in order to highlight the continuity of the teaching given, and to emphasize the importance of the topics recently taken up and their impact on the current life of the Church.

John Paul II has especially brought to light the spousal aspect of the consecration of life by the evangelical counsels, new covenant rooted in that of baptism, enriched by the life and proper charism of each Institute. This consecration is first of all the choice of God, a divine call, a personal vocation to which he or she whom God has chosen, called and drawn to himself responds by the consecration of himself or herself as an act of love. This consecration is an *amen* to God and consecrates the person who is faithful to Him. It is a consecration to God the Father, in Jesus Christ — through Him, with Him and like Him — and to one's brothers, in one love, which brings everything together in God, the Holy Spirit.

Finally, by ever clearer and more insistent references to the new Code of Canon Law, John Paul II wishes to place, as he has said, "the whole Council into the whole life of the Church."

If the Code drew its inspiration from the Council and owes its unity and strength to it, if it has interpreted its teaching in the light of its radiance, seeking to avoid hazardous or false interpretations, then it will enable the entire life of Institutes of consecrated life to be imbued with it.

From the time of its origins, religious life has been meant to be a public witness of a consecrated life totally given to God. Thus it is characterized by separation from the world, by silence which points out its need for contemplation, silence which is not only interior, but exterior as well. The enclosure, proper to every Institute which desires to remain faithful to its origins, is the proof and guarantee of this.

Fraternal life in consecrated life was first of all a gathering of disciples around a spiritual master before becoming, little by little, that community of life and work whose existence and apostolic impact would continue to increase its attraction, power and radiance.

The Pope, since his first address in 1979, has shown himself to be a "master of the Council"; he endeavors to make it known, so that it may be implemented in life, where it must be proclaimed with vigor and uprightness.

The first book of John Paul II's addresses to religious is out of print; the second has been in great demand. The third becomes, like the two preceding ones and along with them, an excellent working tool. Someday these books will form a rich collection. They are recommended to all those who wish to live an authentic consecrated life, to all those who are responsible for the formation of youth and who wish to meet their expectations, to all priests who, through their ministry, are responsible in their own way for the fostering of genuine vocations, to those who aid consecrated persons in a special way to respond faithfully to the grace of their vocation, to the charism of their Institute. These books will help them to better live their consecration to God as an act of love, which is, as John Paul II tells us, a Trinitarian act.

Jean BEYER, S.J.

SYNOPSIS
of the Principal Allocutions
and Letter
of
JOHN PAUL II
to
Religious
1983–1984

Father Jean Beyer, S.J.

ALLOCUTIONS AND LETTER

1983

1984

PERSONS ADDRESSED

A. **To the Plenary Session of the Sacred Congregation for Religious and Secular Institutes:** 42-46.

B. **To the Conferences of Superiors:** 47-53; 144-154.

C. **To Religious Institutes:**
1. Augustinians: 89-97.
2. Capuchins: 179-188; 318-324.
3. Canons Regular of Saint Augustine: 279-287.
4. Carthusians: 237-244; 330-337.
5. Christian Brothers: 196-200.
6. Dominicans: 111-129.
7. Benedictine Family: 298-300; 311-317.
8. Pauline Family (Don Alberione): 36-41.
9. Friars Minor Conventual: 69-77.
10. Hospitaller Order of Saint John of God: 359-365.
11. Society of Jesus: 98-110.
12. Missionary Congregation of the Handmaids of the Holy Spirit: 273-278.
13. Oblates of Saint Frances of Rome: 201-204.
14. Passionists: 325-329.
15. Salesians: 189-195.

D. **To Priests and Men Religious:** 60-68.

E. **To Priests, and Men and Women Religious:** 130-143; 166-178; 205-215; 288-297; 350-358.

F. **To Priests, Men and Women Religious, and Laity:** 216-225; 226-236; 265-272.

G. **To Men Religious, Priests and Brothers:** 24-35.

H. **To Men and Women Religious:** 155-165; 252-264; 338-349.

I. **To Women Religious:** 6-23; 54-59; 78-84; 85-88; 245-251; 301-310.

J. **To Cloistered Religious:** 1-5; 21; 302-307.

SYNOPSIS

I — MAGISTERIUM OF JOHN PAUL II

1. Reference to his allocutions to religious: 30, 51, 101, 105, 146, 183, 244, 253, 323.
2. Reference to other documents:
   a) Redemptor Hominis: 119, 247.
   b) Catechesi Tradendae: 119.
   c) *Redemptionis Donum:* 197, 220, 261-264, 299, 301, 305.
   d) Letter to Priests (Holy Thursday 1979): 182.
   e) Other documents or allocutions: 43, 44, 46, 171, 275, 293.
3. Continuity with Paul VI:
   a) Evangelii Nuntiandi: 26, 48, 106, 119, 145, 152, 347.
   b) *Motu Proprio: Ecclesiae Sanctae:* 255.
   c) Other documents or discourses: 44, 94, 100, 104, 182, 239.
4. Deepening awareness of the Council:
   a) Sacrosanctum Concilium: 55, 257, 282.
   b) Lumen Gentium: 19, 26, 27, 42, 49, 50, 55, 136, 229, 239, 267, 273, 290.
   c) Gaudium et Spes: 42, 61, 181.
   d) Presbyterorum Ordinis: 66, 68, 136, 209, 223, 293.
   e) Optatam Totius: 68, 229.
   f) Perfectae Caritatis: 20, 25, 34, 46, 68, 87, 135, 199, 239, 255, 281, 285, 302, 309, 313, 344.
   g) Apostolicam Actuositatem: 42.
   h) Ad Gentes: 302, 306.
   i) *Dei Verbum:* 314.
   j) *Closing Message of the Council:* 15.
5. *Reference to the Code of Canon Law 1983:* 42, 43, 44, 47, 48, 52, 151, 183, 239, 242.

II — PARTICULAR CHARISM OF EACH INSTITUTE

6. Gift of the Spirit: 18, 29, 43, 227.
7. Specific gift of each Institute: 85, 92, 98, 112, 148, 153, 185, 201, 210, 274, 354.

VI – CONSECRATED LIFE, THEOLOGICAL LIFE

VII — THE EVANGELICAL COUNSELS

53. Three counsels: 10, 82, 263, 309.
54. Consecrated chastity: 109, 137, 206.
55. Evangelical poverty: 109, 206.
56. Filial obedience: 109, 121, 220.
57. Lived in the following of Christ *the Redeemer*: 85, 220, 309, 342.

VIII — CHRIST AND CONSECRATED LIFE

58. *To know Christ:* 53, 312, 314-315.
59. To follow Christ: 10, 25, 51, 85, 107, 113, 310, 312-313, 344.
60. To serve Christ: 107, 344.
61. Union and identification with Christ: 10, 19, 27, 57-58, 68, 107-108, 159, 260, 303, 306, 348.
62. Belonging to Christ: 307.
63. *Christ, the Spouse:* 10, 79, 157, 159, 165, 295, 301, 305.
64. Offering with Christ: 235, 303.
65. Missioned with Christ: 210.
66. Witnesses of Christ, "epiphany" of Christ: 68, 156, 210, 215, 312, 350.
67. Encountering Christ in his brethren: 18, 176, 345, 347, 362.

IX — LIFE IN THE SPIRIT

68. The Spirit, Interior Master, prays and acts in us: 18, 26, 83, 108, 160-162, 236, 274, 276-278, 294, 310.
69. The Spirit, source of unity: 20, 123, 256.
70. Power of the Spirit: 229, 269, 351.
71. Spiritual liberty: 46, 72, 82, 216, 309, 335, 342, 349.
72. *Spiritual joy:* 19, 58, 83, 185, 276, 278, 365.

X — MARY THE MOTHER AND MODEL OF CONSECRATED LIFE

73. Mary leads to Christ: 267, 287.
74. Mother of the Redeemer: 88.
75. *At the center of the plan of salvation:* 139, 140.
76. Star of evangelization, Queen of apostles: 154, 178, 200.

XI — CONSECRATED LIFE AND APOSTOLATE

XII — ACTION AND CONTEMPLATION

XIII — TYPES OF APOSTOLIC ACTION

XIV — TYPOLOGY OF CONSECRATED LIFE

XV — EREMITICAL LIFE

XXV — EXIGENCIES OF RELIGIOUS LIFE

210. Contemplative dimension: 124, 185, 295, 323.
211. Primacy of the spiritual: 72-73, 276.
212. Personal sanctification: 68, 96, 202, 310.
213. Silence and recollection: 126, 132.
214. Prolonged prayer: 19.
215. Time of retreat: 258.
216. Prayer and spiritual vitality: 258, 294.
217. Abnegation, *sense of the cross:* 58, 71, 124, 212, 224-225, 256, 326-327, 349.
218. *Austerity of life:* 96, 109.
219. Humility, *attitude of service:* 177, 256, 354.
220. Daily conversion and the Sacrament of Reconciliation: 27, 52, 107, 182, 258.
221. Evangelical radicalism: 17, 25-26, 35, 145, 149, 309, 349.
222. *Cloister:* 126.
223. Openness to humanity: 50, 344-345.
224. *Solid* and permanent formation: 13, 55-56, 91, 180-183, 323.

XXVI — RULE AND CONSTITUTIONS

225. Expression of the Institute's charism and a sure guide: 34, 186, 203, 325.
226. *Determines and supports the life of prayer:* 295.
227. Renewal: 149, 191, 197, 325.

XXVII — SICK AND INFIRM RELIGIOUS

228. Apostolic fruitfulness: 47- 48, 84, 141-142, 260, 325.
229. *In union with the Savior:* 142, 260.
230. *Irreplaceable ministry:* 142.
231. *Holiness and youthfulness of soul:* 310.

XXVIII — ECCLESIAL VALUE OF THE RELIGIOUS LIFE

232. Visible sign of the Church: 11, 14, 24, 354.
233. Special union with the Church and her mission: 19, 27, 50, 88, 120.
234. Sign of holiness: 48, 87, 120, 145, 295, 354.

235. Sign of communion *and reconciliation:* 16, 20, 24, 28, 52, 109, 151-152, 184, 219-220.
236. *Sign of universality:* 7, 20.
237. Sign of God: 80, 116, 177, 310, 343.
238. Specific role in the Church: 210, 310, 355.
239. Indispensable presence *for the Church and the world:* 35, 86, 164, 175, 213, 261, 296, 308-310.
240. Ecclesial strength: 6, 78, 86, 350.
241. Service of the universal Church: 104-106, 113, 213.
242. In the local Church: 8, 20, 24, 296.
243. Faithfulness to charism and collaboration: 113, 296.
244. Ecclesial awareness, love for the Church: 17, 74-75, 95, 98, 275, 286.
245. Attachment and obedience to the Pope: 9, 33, 102-103, 120, 179.
246. Fidelity and docility to the Magisterium: 17, 33, 50-51, 152, 274.
247. Total availability: 26, 78, 98, 102, 145, 296, 342.
248. Profound identity: 8, 79, 309.
249. Originality of each Institute: richness for the Church: 20, 148, 281.
250. Bi-millenial ecclesial experience: 10.

XXIX — RELIGIOUS LIFE AND SECULAR CLERGY
251. Support and help priests: 78, 302.

XXX — RELIGIOUS SUPERIORSHIP
252. *Important and "pastoral" ministry:* 47.
253. Reminder of spiritual values: 185, 323.
254. Courage and confidence: 48.
255. *Fidelity to the essentials of religious life and to the directives of the Church:* 125-126, 147-149.
256. Role of the General Chapter: 90, 98-100, 113, 125, 197, 273.
257. Conferences of religious superiors: 52, 144, 147, 154.
258. *Federations, unions:* 255, 279, 286.

XXXI — NEW FORMS OF RELIGIOUS LIFE
259. With fidelity to the Church: 51.
260. *Necessary* climate of prayer: 51.

287. Particularisms and divisions: 51, 151-152, 353.
288. *Deviations or manipulations of the Gospel:* 17.
289. Horizontalism: 73, 202.

XXXIV — SECULARIZATION
290. Secularization: 94, 105, 149, 191.
291. Questioning *or attenuating* one's identity: 30, 51, 126, 148-149, 281, 352, 355.
292. *Reducing the mission of the Church to a temporal salvation:* 106.

XXXV — VOCATION–DIVINE CALL
293. Divine call: 85, 166, 247.
294. *Call of the Spirit:* 106, 160-162.
295. Call of Christ to follow him: 27, 261, 335.
296. Call renewed throughout one's life: 161.
297. Sign of predilection: 246, 309.
298. *Call of a "spousal" love:* 161, 261.
299. Gratuitous call: 79, 246.
300. Special call to holiness: 160.

XXXVI — RESPONSE TO THE CALL
301. *Act of confidence in divine assistance:* 247.
302. Free response: 159, 247, 262, 309.
303. Response of love: 79.
304. Radical option: 33, 228.
305. *Definitive decision:* 247.
306. *Joy and seriousness of the engagement:* 246.
307. Fidelity to the call: 227, 356.
308. Response lived with joy: 6, 19, 87, 177, 264, 310, 342, 349.
309. Fidelity to God: 250.
310. *Fidelity to Christ and the Church:* 19, 35.
311. Thanksgiving for the call received: 54, 79, 161, 166.

XXXVII — AWAKENING OF VOCATIONS
312. *Fear of definitive engagements:* 248, 254.
313. *Generosity of youth:* 48, 106, 254, 324, 335.
314. Attracted by fidelity: 34, 48, 54, 106, 310.
315. Attracted by radicalism: 254, 335.

XLV — PRIESTLY VOCATION

XLVI — SECULAR INSTITUTES

JOHN PAUL II
Speaks to Religious
Principal Allocutions and Letter
1983–1984

1

TO CLOISTERED RELIGIOUS IN GRECCIO

January 2, 1983

1.   On the joyous occasion of my visit to Greccio and in the mystic and gentle atmosphere of this locality, so intimately Franciscan and therefore Christian, I am very pleased to be able to address a particularly cordial greeting to you, cloistered religious, assembled here to meet me, remembering and imitating well the love and the veneration toward the Roman Pontiff that Saint Francis always felt and taught.

2.   Moved by your presence, so affectionate and significant, I thank you; and I also wish to express to you again the sentiments I feel for your total consecration to the contemplative life. This gift of yours to the Absolute, which requires a vocation and which uniquely has Love as its ideal, is a typical way of "being the Church," of living in the Church, of accomplishing the illuminating and saving mission of the Church. I intend to emphasize strongly the essential value of your presence in the providential plan of Redemption and to confirm you in the validity of your proposals of prayer and penance for the salvation of mankind.

3.   Your ideal is first of all a "sign" for modern man who is troubled by thousands of problems and tormented by so many social and political events. Cloistered nuns, with their life of prayer and austerity, propose to the world the words of Jesus: "Seek out instead his kingship over you, and the rest will follow in turn" (Lk 12:31); and the words of the Letter to the Hebrews: "For here we have no lasting city; we are seeking the one which is to come" (Heb 13:14). Your real and concrete example therefore becomes an

34

exhortation and an invitation to man to re-enter himself, to leave superficiality, dissipation, the hunger for efficiency; to feel that in effect our heart—as Saint Augustine said— is made for the Infinite, and it finds peace and rest only in him. For you the words that Saint Teresa of Jesus wrote in her autobiography are also of value: "After having seen the great vision of the Lord, there was no longer anyone who in comparison would seem so pleasing to me as to occupy my mind any longer. . ." (*Life,* 37, 4). This is the continual challenge which, by your choice, you throw out to the world.

4.   Your total consecration to Love is also a warning for all Christians, for priests, religious, theologians, and leaders of the Church. Certainly, for the proclamation of the Gospel and for the salvation of souls, the various means of the apostolate are necessary: the search for new methods, creativity, novelty, active dynamism, updating ideas and proposals. . .But personal prayer, the entreaty for light and strength for oneself and for the entire world, remains essential, just as the fundamental concern must always be the maintenance and the defense of the "deposit" of truth which Jesus, by being born in Bethlehem, revealed and then entrusted to the Church.

5.   Being a few months away from the beginning of the commemorative Jubilee of Christ's Redemption, I entrust to you, dearest cloistered sisters, the successful outcome of this initiative, which I feel so necessary for reflection and conversion. I entrust to your prayers and to your spiritual fervor the entire Jubilee Year, and in a particular way, two events which are near to my heart: the Italian National Eucharistic Congress, and the Synod of Bishops on the theme "Reconciliation and Penance."

May the Divine Savior always fill you with the holy joy which Saint Francis of Assisi felt here at Greccio! May the holy Virgin and Saint Joseph accompany you with their heavenly protection! And may my Apostolic Blessing, which I heartily impart to you, help you.

2

TO WOMEN RELIGIOUS IN COSTA RICA

March 3, 1983

6.   I respond with deep gratitude and profound affection
to the warm welcome which you have given me in
this metropolitan Cathedral of San Jose, where I know that
members of the clergy, men and women religious, and seminarians are united. You are the elect part of the Church
in Costa Rica, its most precious and necessary vital forces.
I express to you my most profound appreciation for your
state of life and your activity. I encourage you to continue
in your fidelity to the Lord without hesitation, with joy and
optimism. I want to tell you that I pray for your needs and
intentions, and I bless you with all my heart. In particular, I pray for the perseverance and the good training of the
seminarians, who are the future ministers of the Church.
        Since I will be speaking specifically to the priests
in Salvador, and to the male religious in Guatemala, today I wish to address the sisters in particular.

7.   Dear sisters consecrated to Jesus Christ and to his
Kingdom, I see you in the variety of apostolic commitments of your various Institutes and in their presence
in the individual countries. Some of you are from the peoples of Central America, Belize or Haiti, where I am carrying out my apostolic visit; others come from the remaining
nations of the American continent or have come from other
continents. However, I know that all of you feel that you
fit in well in these lands which are your spiritual homeland,
and thus you give a dimension of universality to the holy
Church.

8.   I have the joy of perceiving that you are enthusias-
        tic about the ideals of the Church which lives in
these lands, because one of the characteristics of your
presence must be the deep penetration into the particular
Churches, where you provide a precious help to evangelization, enlivening the parish communities and ecclesial
groups; you are authentic collaborators of your pastors, who
appreciate your work, and of the faithful, who with their
love and respect help you keep strong both your identity
as consecrated people and your commitment to those in
most need.

9.   During this meeting of faith, prayer, and spiritual
        communion with Peter's Successor, to whom your
consecration binds you in affection, obedience and apostolic
collaboration, my words are intended to bring you a message of joy and hope to confirm your identity and open up
new paths for your ecclesial commitment, now strengthened by my presence among you.

10.   As the Church has always done with regard to Chris-
        tian virgins since the earliest days of Christianity,
I would like to remind you of *your bond with Jesus Christ,*
your Lord and Spouse, whose love and whose cause you have
embraced at the same time.
        You are disciples because you have followed him by
the evangelical counsels of chastity, poverty and obedience.
Along with Saint Paul, you can say: "For to me, 'life' means
Christ" (Phil 1:21), because you have personally consecrated yourselves to him and you have been called to feel
this communion of love fully, so as to be able to say that
it is he who lives in you and who communicates true life
to you. *You have identified yourselves with his cause* and for
this reason, leaving everything behind, as the apostles did,
you have chosen to be witnesses of the values and obligations of the Kingdom.

11.   Your contribution is very precious to the Church. I
        know that you enthusiastically bear a good part of
the burden of many parochial activities, of evangelization,

of teaching, of works of mercy, of community animation, of ecclesial presence and witness among the poorest, the alienated, the needy; with the ability to make the Church present with an authentically maternal appearance, with sensitivity and affection, with wisdom and balance. In this dimension you feel the joy of the consecration through which you can say, paraphrasing the words of Saint Paul: *For me, "life" is being the Church.*

12.   At a moment in history when woman is acquiring in society a place which belongs to her, with an advancement which gives her dignity, I see with satisfaction your qualified presence as messengers and witnesses of the Gospel. This movement, which is now acquiring greater form of expression in the pastoral community, has its foundation and roots in the very attitude of the Teacher towards the women who followed him (cf. Lk 23:55), who enjoyed his friendship, like Martha and Mary of Bethany (cf. Jn 12:1-8), and who were messengers of his Resurrection, like Mary Magdelen (cf. Jn 20:18), or who were invited to recognize him as the Messiah, like the Samaritan woman (cf. Jn 4:39).

13.   The Church also entrusts to you the service of the Word and catechesis, education in the faith, cultural and human advancement; she requires of you an adequate preparation, always more intense, therefore, in biblical and dogmatic theology, liturgy, spirituality and science; and at the same time she recognizes with what enthusiasm and generosity you bring the Gospel to the poor, to the most simple, and to the restless youth of this geographical area.

14.   However, the Gospel is life, and in your heart, consecrated to Christ, you carry the instinct for life, for charity—which is the very life of God—which takes on flesh in the works of welfare and advancement. The Christians of these lands rightly claim your irreplaceable presence near the sickbed, in school, in the various manifestations of the evangelical mercy proper to religious creativity. In these places, in these environments, you are the *very*

presence of the love of Christ, you are the *face of the Church,* which shines before men through his love, translated into goodness, help, consolation, liberation and hope.

15.   Looking concretely at the situation of your peoples, the restlessness which agitates society, the fragile balance of peace, the commitments to promote justice which is yet to be realized, I can do no less than reaffirm my confidence in your mission.

        At this time, I would like to reecho the words of the Second Vatican Council in its Message to Women: "You, consecrated virgins, in a world where egoism and the search for pleasure would become law, be the guardians of purity, unselfishness and piety. . .you to whom life is entrusted at this grave moment in history, it is for you to save the peace of the world."[1]

16.   Your mission could seem to be too exacting for you, too great for your abilities. In many cases, since you are near the people, you hold in your hands the education of children, young people and adults; by nature and evangelical mission, you must be sowers of peace and concord, of unity and fraternity; you can disengage the mechanisms of violence through an integral education and a promotion of man's authentic values; your consecrated life must be a challenge to egoism and oppression, a call to conversion, a factor of reconciliation among men.

17.   To be able duly to fulfill this mission, remain firm in the radical nature of your faith, in the love of Christ and in ecclesial awareness. You will thus avoid possible deviations or manipulations of the Gospel in the necessary preferential, but not exclusive, option in favor of the poor.

        Do not let yourselves be deceived by party ideologies; do not succumb to the temptations of choices which one day could cost you the price of your freedom. Have confidence in your pastors and always be in communion with them. In this communion with the Church, in an identification with its guiding principles, you will find the norm for sure action. Collaborate also in discerning the reality upon which the light of the Gospel must fall. Almost through supernatural instinct, always direct the authenticity of your apostolic choices with the compass *of the direction of the Church,* composed of *sincere communion with its Magisterium,* in unity with its pastors.

18.   With this guarantee, embrace the cause of the poor; *be present where Christ suffers in his needy brothers;* arrive with your generosity in places where only the love of Christ knows how to perceive the lack of a friendly presence. Be patient and generous in the hope of a better society, sowing the seed of a new humanity which builds rather than destroys, which transforms the negative into the positive, as an announcement of resurrection.

The Holy Spirit, who has stirred up the charism of religious life in the Church and has also stirred up the charism of each one of your Institutes, will give you light and creativity to know how to incarnate it into new values and new situations, with the impulsion of evangelical newness which every charism inspired by the Spirit possesses when it remains in ecclesial communion.

19.   As points of this meeting for you to reflect on, I want to leave you some reasons for fidelity which will broaden your heart and give you the full joy of an authentic disciple of Jesus, even in the midst of persecution, lack of understanding, the apparent ineffectiveness of your apostolic efforts.

First of all, *fidelity to Christ,* through loving communion with him through prayer, for which you must reserve long and frequent periods in your life, however much apostolic necessities may press upon you. Your prayer must seek the experience of Christ, followed, loved and served.

Fidelity also *to the Church.* Your consecration unites you to the Church in a special way (cf. *Lumen Gentium,* 44); and in perfect communion with her, with her mission, with her pastors and her faithful, you will find the full meaning of your religious life. As consecrated women, continue to be the honor of Mother Church.

40

Carry her sorrows and pains in your heart and in your life; be capable of reflecting at every moment the evangelical countenance of the Spouse of Christ.

20.   Remain united *in fidelity to your own charism.* In this way, the Church shows the beauty of the various evangelical expressions assumed by your Founders and Foundresses. In communion with your Institutes, you contribute a universal dimension to the particular Churches, a dimension which your religious families have. By living in communion with your sisters, you realize that first communion which assures the presence of Jesus in your midst and guarantees a community's apostolic fruitfulness (cf. *Perfectae Caritatis,* 15).

Live in communion, also, with the various Institutes, in order to offer the People of God the example of an evangelical unity which reflects the union of the Mystical Body, where all the charisms are united by the same Spirit.

Finally, be *faithful to your people, to your particular Churches,* to their efforts and to their hopes for justice and advancement, so that the Church may appear with you completely incarnate in the various nations, in their characteristics, in their values and traditions, in the ambience of the one, holy and catholic Church.

21.   All that I have wanted to entrust to you has its suitable application, respecting the kind of life proper to them, *to the religious of a contemplative life.* By their lives, they silently give witness to the value of union with God, of penance, and of total sacrifice. With their prayer they embrace the needs of the poor, they assume the concerns of the universal Church and of the particular communities. They are the tangible manifestation of the fact that your peoples have an authentic contemplative capacity.

22.   The consecrated persons who in the midst of society live their commitment of animation, *according to the characteristics of the secular Institutes,* also will be able to make their own the points I wanted to give, accenting their presence in society, particularly in the specific environments of their apostolate.

23. Dear sisters: I cannot leave you without showing you the perfect model of this fidelity which I have just asked of you: the Virgin Mary. In her you will find the first disciple and the first consecrated woman. She is the model of contemplation, of proclamation of the Word, of presence in the midst of her people. She is the expression of all the charisms and the Mother of all the consecrated.

Your peoples are devoted to Our Lady and perceive in the preaching of the Gospel the mark of catholicity *when she is spoken of,* or its absence *if she is not spoken of.* By loving the Virgin, by speaking of her, you will enter into the heart of your people. Above all, however, if you know how to reflect her in your life, you will be these *qualified messengers of the Gospel* which the Church in Central America needs.

May she keep you faithful to the Gospel. I entrust you to her, so that with your word and your life you may be able to say to everyone, only and always: "Jesus Christ is the Lord." Amen.

---

[1] "Message to Women," at the closing of the Council, December 8, 1965, (8,11).

3

TO MEN RELIGIOUS IN GUATEMALA

March 7, 1983

24.   Today this National Expiatory Sanctuary of the Sacred Heart is the meeting place of the Pope with the men religious of the whole geographical area which I am visiting these days. However, there are also priests, sisters and seminarians here from Guatemala. These are the vital centers of Church life in this nation. I therefore address to everyone my thought full of esteem, my most affectionate and grateful greeting, my word of encouragement for your dedication to Christ and for your ecclesial vocation, along with my special blessing.

Dear brothers, I have saved a special meeting to be able to be with you. First of all I wish to express my gratitude to you for your ecclesial presence in this land, where you are in the service of particular Churches.

Many of you are sons of this land. Others have come from near and far. But all of you are urged on by the *same love for these peoples* from whom you have also received much, through their simple faith, their sincere life of piety, their generous affection.

The special situations which these people are living and their very closeness favor an intense communion between you. For my part, I would like to encourage the efforts for ecclesial communion, for collaboration with your bishops, for the search for your better insertion into the ecclesial life in these sister nations, in order to be, as religious, *a sign of communion and reconciliation.*

25.   You are committed to making the supreme rule of your life the following of Christ according to the Gospel (cf. *Perfectae Caritatis,* 2, a). Allow me to remind you

of this: you must be *specialists of Jesus' Gospel,* vitally identified with his words and with his example.

The distinctive mark of religious life in the Church must consist in maintaining the purity of the Gospel not only in the *vows* which are characteristic of your consecration, but above all in *perfect charity* towards God and your neighbor, which is the essence of the Gospel; in the *Beatitudes* which affirm their originality with respect to the mentality of the world, and in these specific manifestations of the Gospel which are the *charisms* of your Founders.

26.   Fidelity to the Gospel assures the vitality of religious life, of which my predecessor Paul VI opportunely spoke: "Thanks to their consecration they are eminently willing and free to leave everything and to go and proclaim the Gospel even to the ends of the earth. They are enterprising and their apostolate is often marked by an originality, by a genius that demands admiration. They are generous: often they are found at the outposts of the mission, and they take the greatest risks for their health and their very lives" (*Evangelii Nuntiandi,* 69).

Thus, be faithful to the perennial youthfulness of the Gospel which Christ has entrusted to the life-giving action of the Holy Spirit and of his charisms (cf. *Lumen Gentium,* 4).

27.   The awareness of your *consecration to Christ in the Church* is a guarantee of fidelity. Yes, one does not embrace the Gospel merely as a just cause or as a utopia. *The Gospel is a person:* it is Jesus Christ, the Lord. He who "was handed over to death for our sins and raised up for our justification" (Rom 4:25). He has called you to follow him to the Cross; and one cannot follow him with fidelity, if one does not first of all love him deeply. For this, religious consecration vitally unites you to Jesus Christ and becomes a bond of love which requires friendship and communion with him, nourished by the sacraments, especially the Eucharist and Penance, by the meditation of his Word, by prayer, by identification with his very sentiments.

Embracing the counsels for the Kingdom of heaven means serving the Kingdom of Christ, which is the Church. Thus, religious life directly signifies a bond "with the Church and her mystery" and is developed for its benefit (cf. *Lumen Gentium,* 44).

28.   However, always remember that in Christ's plan one cannot conceive of religious life as being independent of the bishops, or as indifferent to the hierarchy, because there cannot be charisms except in the service of communion and the unity of the Body of Christ (cf. 1 Cor 12:4-11). Consequently, not only must *any type of apostolate or magisterium parallel to that of the bishops* be excluded, but it must also be emphasized that it is the very nature of religious life by all means to increase communion, to promote it in the faithful, to solidify it where it loses vigor. This has been the characteristic which all the Founders have evidenced.

29.   Yes, dear religious. I know that when I mention the Founders of your Institutes you feel within you this type of "family spirit" which identifies you with them and with your brothers. It is the feeling that the charism is something alive, vital, animated by the Spirit, made flesh and blood in your experience of formation and of religious life.

You are the trustees and the ones responsible for this "experience of the Spirit" which is the charism of the Founders. You are the *sons of these "men of the Spirit," their living presence* in the Church of today, in this land.

The faithful recognize you by your union with these saints. And these same faithful expect *you to be and act as true sons of these saints;* united with God, and through him, committed to promoting justice, to elevating man culturally and humanly, in the cause of the poor. Remember, however, that in working first of all on their behalf, you must not exclude anyone.

30.   One cannot think of the Founders' work without seeing in them the incarnation of the Gospel, as *extend-
ing through the geography and the history of the Church.*

From this clear evangelical perspective, they offer
you the example of a presence alongside the people and
their suffering. Without allowing themselves to be carried
away by temptations or currents of a political nature, they
are a valid example for you even today, because, as I said
to the priests and religious of Mexico, "you are not social
directors, political leaders or officials of a temporal
power."[1] Your Founders were able to embody Christ's charity effectively, not only with words, but with generous
gestures, with services and institutions. In this way they
have left a trace in history, they have made culture, they
have sown truth and life, from which we continue to gather
the fruits.

This remembrance, my dear brothers, allows me to
ask you for *complete fidelity to the Gospel and to the spirit
of your Founders,* so that, today as yesterday, you, religious,
might live in perfect charity with a profound sense of faith,
with generous dedication to the task of evangelization,
which is the first task entrusted to you, without ever per-
mitting manipulating ideological motivations to replace
your evangelical identity or inspire your action, which *must
always be that of men of the Church.* Starting from this clear
conviction, also work with enthusiasm for man's dignity.

31.   With this evangelical charity which, as your
Founders demonstrated, *is the most concrete and
complete of any human ideology,* and which concerns itself
with man in his spiritual, material and social dimension,
I exhort you to renew the fervor of your life and your works.
The children of the Church who live in this land ask this
of you. They want to feel that you are near, *first of all as
spiritual guides,* as specialists in Christ's charity, which
urges one to love others and to commit oneself with all one's
strength for man's justice and dignity.

The tasks of evangelization and of the formation
of the Christian communities are before your eyes. With
your generosity, make up for the lack of vocations or for

distances between ecclesial groups, so much more in need of your presence the farther away they are from the great urban or rural centers. Also educate popular piety so that it might bear the fruits of that simple and generous faith which animates it.

32.   Continue to train a mature laity that will responsibly assume its place in the Church and give itself with clear-sightedness to the mission which belongs to it: to transform civil society from within. And give to the poor first of all—as I indicated to you before—the bread of the Word, the defense of their rights when they are oppressed, advancement, integral education and every possible assistance which will help them live with dignity. In this, follow the indications of the Church's social teaching just as she proposes it and have confidence in this social teaching of the Church. The times in which we live give us historic proof of its validity.

33.   I ask you to give particular attention to youth. Your young people are generous; they expect the sympathy and the help of those who have received from their Founders a special mission of Christian, cultural, technical, and human education. Therefore, may your presence not be missing from education centers of all levels, where the values which form those who one day will rule the destinies of your peoples are determined.

        In this important field, as in all your apostolic activity—as an individual, as a religious community or Institute, or as associates in the widest sense—faithfully follow the directions of your bishops and demonstrate your love for the Church by the respect, communion and collaboration which they deserve as the pastors of the particular Churches. Through them you will be united with the visible head of the Church, to whom Christ entrusted the charism of confirming his brothers in the faith. Also be generous in helping and collaborating with the diocesan clergy.

        With these requests the Pope renews his confidence in you, he encourages you toward a fruitful growth in your charisms and towards an enthusiastic dedication which must be the distinctive sign of your radical option for Christ, for the Church, and for man, our brother.

34.   Do you want a key to apostolic fruitfulness? Live unity, the source of a great apostolic strength (cf. *Perfectae Caritatis,* 15). In fraternal communion there is, in fact, the guarantee of the presence of Christ and of his Spirit, in order to put your responsibilities into practice, following the rules of your Institutes.

The Church needs the example and the witness of religious who live *evangelical brotherhood.* The groups and communities await encouragement based on your experience of the communion of goods, of common prayer, of reciprocal help.

The young people who knock on your doors want to find an ecclesial life that is characterized by the *fervor of prayer,* by the *family spirit,* by *apostolic commitment.* These young people are sensitive to community values and expect to find them in religious life. Be capable of welcoming them and guiding them, carefully cultivating new vocations; their search must be one of your principal concerns.

35.   My dear brothers: all of your Institutes profess a special love for the Virgin Mary; under various titles and with various emphases, the Virgin appears as the reflection of a living Gospel, and therefore as the Mother of all religious. In her name I ask that you be able to maintain mutual appreciation for your charisms and collaboration in your apostolic works.

I entrust you to her, to preserve and increase your fidelity to Christ and to the Church. I ask her for the flowering and perseverance of abundant vocations for your religious families. The Church of this geographical area needs your presence, to live this fullness of the Gospel which belongs to religious life. May Mary, the Virgin who is faithful and solicitous about man's needs, grant you this grace. Amen.

---

[1] January 27, 1979. Cf. Book I—no. 68.

48

4

TO THE MEN AND WOMEN RELIGIOUS OF
THE SAINT PAUL SOCIETY IN ROME

March 21, 1983

36.   To welcome the Pauline Family by receiving you, beloved brothers and sisters, is cause for great joy for
me. And not only because of the present circumstance,
although so significant, which has inspired this meeting—
namely, to commemorate the beginning of the centenary
of the birth of your Founder, Don Giacomo Alberione, and
to celebrate the twenty-fifth or the fiftieth anniversary of
the ordination or the religious profession of many of his sons
and daughters—but also because of a general reason: a
more direct contact and a more intense communion *"in fide
et caritate"* between each one of you and the Successor of
Peter.
        The Paulines are now present throughout the world
with their multiple works, with their apostolic initiatives,
with the creativity of their achievements in the vast sector of the social communications media. You are a living
part of the Church and it is therefore natural that you not
only be recognized, but followed and encouraged in your
fruitful ministry by the one in the Church who has the
gravest responsibility in regard to fulfilling the supreme
mandate of Christ: "Go into all the world and preach the
Gospel to the whole creation" (Mk 16:15); "Go therefore and
make disciples of all nations..." (Mt 28:19).

37.   *A tree with many branches:* glancing through the lists
of the various Institutes, Congregations, and Associations into which the Pauline Family is divided and to
which the ardent soul of the Founder gave rise with inexhaustible fruitfulness, I believe that this can be its most
appropriate and comprehensive definition. It is a tree with

many branches since, from the first Congregation of Pauline Priests and Disciples which sprang up in long ago August 1914 to the most recent Congregation of the Apostoline Sisters, founded towards the end of the 1950's, it has nine "branches" to which can also be added the numerous and flourishing associations of alumni. And I am pleased to recall here that one of these branches, the Pious Disciples of the Divine Master, has a community at the service of the Holy See in the Vatican.

It is a tree, because in this multiplicity of offshoots the original trunk was and remains one and—what is more important—the vital sap which nourishes it and makes it develop is one. In fact, unvaried and constant was the idea that gradually inspired Don Alberione to study and put into effect all possible ways of penetration and new modes of presence in the strata of modern society in order to make room in it for the Gospel. It was precisely this search, lasting the entire span of his long life, which made him very dear to the Supreme Pontiffs and in a special way—as is known—to my predecessor Paul VI.

38. In naming his foundations after Saint Paul, your father evidently did not limit himself to an onomastic or verbal choice, but intended to go back to the unmistakable spirit and style of the Apostle of the Gentiles. In fact, Don Alberione wanted to take from Saint Paul not only his name or merely his patronage, but also and above all ideal inspiration and spiritual nourishment, proposing to himself and to those who already followed him in his earliest initiatives, just as to you who follow him in the present, *the outline of an open, up-to-date, modern apostolate,* according to the teachings and the examples of the Apostle himself. As Paul was always in search of new forms and courageous methods for proclaiming Christ and his mystery to the Gentiles (cf. Eph 3:2-10)—and in this context his missionary journeys, his letters, and his tireless dedication can be placed—it is thus worthwhile for you to look to him willingly to confirm yourselves in your specific vocation and to persevere in your commitment to original, generous action, with no sparing of effort or sacrifices.

39.   It is therefore obvious that the interior sap which must nourish your ministry in the Church and in society is the charity of the truth revealed by Christ and entrusted by him to the apostles and their successors, and that is, to the Church, which is its guarantor and transmits it and defends it with its authentic and permanent Magisterium.

40.   But there is a sector to which the Paulines are dedicated with particular commitment: that of the press, for the preparation and distribution of editions of books and periodicals with a Christian orientation and therefore corresponding to a pedagogical-formative purpose. This sector is extremely vast and important since on the one hand it extends to and is linked with the audio-visual sector, and on the other hand it very closely touches—notably in relation to so many things produced which are morally equivocal and damaging—the problem of the Christian education of youth.

    Your mission in the specific field of publishing is of extreme relevance and necessity. May your ideal and your concern always be predominantly that of human, Christian and Catholic formation. Yours is a true evangelical-ecclesial mission: it is for this that you have been called, following the footsteps of Don Alberione.

    May his lofty example serve to inspire and sustain you in a vigilant and active, disinterested and generous commitment, always inspired by an authentic evangelical spirit.

41.   In the sector of social communications—as in all others—may you always be animated by an authentic apostolic spirit so that your constant guide may be not the criteria of profit or of other advantages of a temporal nature that a particular initiative may produce, but solely that of the good which it may sow in society.

    At the beginning I defined your family as *"a tree of many branches":* this is no more than a recognition of what you are and represent. But I want to conclude with a wish: in strengthened fidelity to the spirit and to the directives

of your Founder I hope that, through the multiplicity of initiatives and the wealth of good results, it may be also and
above all a *"tree bearing much fruit"!*
 With my Apostolic Blessing.

5

TO THE PLENARY ASSEMBLY OF
THE SACRED CONGREGATION FOR
RELIGIOUS AND SECULAR INSTITUTES

May 6, 1983

42.   I thank you for your presence and I express to you my joy at this meeting, and my gratitude for the work that you do to inspire and foster consecrated life. The evangelical counsels, in fact, are a "divine gift which the Church has received from her Lord and which she ever preserves with the help of his grace" (*Lumen Gentium,* 43), and therefore what is done in the Congregation on behalf of their profession is extremely sound and valuable.

The plenary assembly which you are concluding today was held along this line of inspiring and fostering consecrated life. You have taken into particular consideration the identity and the mission of those Institutes which, because of their distinctive mission *"in saeculo et ex saeculo"* (Can. 713, par. 2—New Code), are called "secular Institutes."

It is the first time that one of your plenary assemblies has dealt with them directly: therefore it was a timely choice, which the promulgation of the new Code has inspired. The secular Institutes—which in 1947 received ecclesial recognition with the Apostolic Constitution *Provida Mater* issued by my predecessor, Pius XII—now find in the Code their rightful place on the basis of the doctrine of the Second Vatican Council. In fact, these Institutes are intended to be faithful expressions of that ecclesiology which the Council reconfirms when it emphasizes the universal vocation to holiness (cf. *Lumen Gentium,* Chap. 5), the inherent tasks of the baptized (cf. *Lumen Gentium,* Chap. 4; *Apostolicam Actuositatem*), the Church's presence in the world in which she must act as leaven and be the "universal sacrament of salvation" (*Lumen Gentium,* 48; cf. *Gaudium et Spes*), the variety and the dignity of the various vocations, and the "particular honor" which the Church pays towards "total continence embraced on behalf of the Kingdom of heaven" (*Lumen Gentium,* 42) and towards the witness of evangelical poverty and obedience (*ibid.*).

43.   Quite rightly your reflection dwelt on the constitutive, theological and juridical elements of the secular Institutes, keeping in mind the formulation of the canons dedicated to them in the recently promulgated Code, and examining them in the light of the teaching which Pope Paul VI, and I myself with the discourse of August 28, 1980, have confirmed in audiences granted them.

We must express profound gratitude to the Father of infinite mercy, who has taken to heart the needs of mankind and, with the life-giving power of the Spirit, has undertaken in this century new initiatives for mankind's redemption. Honor and glory be to the triune God for this outpouring of grace which the secular Institutes are, through which he manifests the inexhaustible benevolence with which the Church herself loves the world in the name of her God and Lord.

The newness of the gift which the Spirit has made to the Church's everlasting fruitfulness in response to the needs of our times is grasped only if its constituent elements in their inseparability are well understood: consecration and secularity; the consequent apostolate of witness, of Christian commitment in social life and of evangelization; the fraternity which, without being determined by a community of life, is truly communion; the external lifestyle itself, which is not separate from the environment in which it may appear.

44.   Now it is necessary to know and make known this vocation that is so relevant and, I should say, so urgent, the vocation of persons who consecrate themselves to God by practicing the evangelical counsels and strive to immerse their whole lives and all their activities in

that special consecration, creating in themselves a total availability to the Father's will and working to change the world from within (cf. Discourse of August 28, 1980).

The promulgation of the new Code will surely allow this better knowledge, but it must also urge pastors to foster among the faithful an understanding which is not approximate or yielding, but exact and respectful of the qualifying characteristics of secular Institutes.

In this way, generous responses to this difficult but beautiful vocation of "full consecration to God and to souls" (cf. *Primo Feliciter,* 5) are aroused: a demanding vocation, because one responds to it by carrying the baptismal commitments to the most perfect consequences of evangelical radicalism, and also because this evangelical life must be embodied in the most diverse situations.

In fact, the variety of the gifts entrusted to the secular Institutes expresses the various apostolic aims which embrace all areas of human and Christian life. This pluralistic wealth is also shown in the numerous spiritualities which animate the secular Institutes, with the diversity of the holy bonds which characterize various modes of practicing the evangelical counsels and the great possibilities of their incorporation in all areas of social life. My predecessor, Pope Paul VI, who showed so much affection for the secular Institutes, rightly said that if they "remain faithful to their vocation, they will be like an experimental laboratory in which the Church tests the concrete modes of its relations with the world" (Paul VI, *Discourse to the International Congress of Secular Institutes,* August 25, 1976). Therefore, lend your support to these Institutes that they may be faithful to the original charisms of their foundation recognized by the hierarchy, and be alert to discover in their fruits the teaching which God wants to give us for the life and action of the entire Church.

45. If there is a development and strengthening of the secular Institutes, the local Churches will also benefit.

This aspect has been kept in mind during your plenary assembly, also because various episcopates, through the suggestions given with regard to your meeting, have pointed out that the relationship between secular Institutes and local Churches is worthy of being deepened.

Even while respecting their characteristics, the secular Institutes must understand and adopt the pastoral urgencies of the particular Churches, and encourage their members to live the hopes and toils, the projects and concerns, the spiritual riches and limitations with diligent participation; in a word, to live in communion with their concrete Church. This must be a point for greater reflection by the secular Institutes, just as it must be a concern of the pastors to recognize and request their contribution according to their proper nature.

In particular, another responsibility rests on the pastors: that of offering the secular Institutes all the doctrinal wealth they need. They want to be part of the world and ennoble temporal realities, setting them in order and elevating them, that all things may be brought into one under Christ's headship (cf. Eph 1:10). Therefore, may all the wealth of Catholic doctrine on creation, incarnation and redemption be given to these Institutes that they may make their own God's wise and mysterious plans for man, for history and for the world.

46.   Beloved brothers and sons and daughters! It is with a sentiment of true esteem and also of deep encouragement for the secular Institutes that today I have taken the opportunity offered me by this meeting to emphasize some aspects treated by you during the past few days.

I hope that your plenary assembly may fully achieve the goal of offering to the Church better information on the secular Institutes and helping them live their vocation in awareness and fidelity.

May this Jubilee Year of the Redemption, which calls everyone to "a renewed discovery of the love of God who gives himself" (Apostolic Bull, *Aperite Portas Redemptori,* 8) and a renewed encounter with the merciful goodness of God, be particularly for consecrated persons also a renewed and pressing invitation to follow "with greater freedom" and "more closely" (*Perfectae Caritatis*, 1) the Master who calls them to the pathways of the Gospel.

May the Virgin Mary be a constant and sublime model to them, and may she always guide them with her motherly protection.

With these sentiments, I gladly impart my intercessory Apostolic Blessing to you here present and to those enrolled in the secular Institutes throughout the world.

6

TO THE INTERNATIONAL ASSEMBLY OF SUPERIORS GENERAL IN ROME

May 13, 1983

47.   Accept my most heartfelt greeting! It is always a reason for joy for me to meet with female religious and to express openly the Church's deep esteem for their lives of total consecration to the Lord, the keen interest and the confidence which the Holy See has in them and their mission.

But today's meeting assumes an altogether special importance because of its very universal nature: in fact, in the persons of the Superiors General of the various religious Institutes spread throughout the world, there is expressed, in a certain way, the presence in Rome of all female religious and their desire to attest to their devotion to the Church and to the Pope, and to accept personally his teachings and directives.

Therefore, through you, I send a heartfelt special blessing to all the female religious in the world: to the contemplatives; to those who in humble generosity are dedicated to the service of the brethren; to those tried by age, by sickness of body or mind. The sacrifices of all of them have an incomparable value in the eyes of the Lord.

To you, gathered in Rome to examine the "Apostolic Spirituality of Religious," I want above all to offer a word of encouragement and comfort, which is required by such an important, such a delicate, but at the same time such a pastoral mission, conferred on you by your very election: that of building up in Christ a fraternal community where, above all, God may be sought and loved (cf. Canon 619).

48.   The theme of your works, in preparation for some years, is rich in teachings and offers you the oppor-

tunity not only to treat of your apostolic activities, but even more to draw from the sources which must nourish them.

Moreover, I strongly advise you to meditate on the teachings of the new Code of Canon Law bearing on this subject. It will offer you valuable insights into a fundamental part of your lives.

In fact, the Code recalls in the first place (cf. Canon 673) that the apostolate of religious consists above all in giving witness to their consecrated lives, nourished by prayer and penance. This basic affirmation is of particular importance since it places the apostolic role of religious in its true place. Precisely through their innermost beings they join the dynamism of the Church, thirsty for the absolute of God, called to sanctity. Above all, they are called to witness this sanctity (cf. *Evangelii Nuntiandi*, 69).

Before being translated into *proclamation* or action, the apostolate is the revelation of God present in the apostle. And this revelation postulates that the religious be in intimate and constant contact with the Lord. In this way, it matters little whether she be in the fullness of her strength or infirm, young or of advanced age, active or without any direct activity: evangelization is real and deep to the degree that Christ's life is reflected through her personal life. The great evangelizers were primarily prayerful souls, interior souls: they always knew how to find the time for prolonged contemplation.

At this historical moment when you all have reason to suffer from the lack of apostolic workers, it is especially well to pause and meditate on this truth, in the faith that "being" has more value than "doing," which is always limited and imperfect. Moreover, be certain that your courageous and joyful fidelity to the fundamental demands of consecrated life will offer a pressing invitation to young women, always ready to be generous, to follow the Lord along the path marked out by you.

49. In this perspective, although they are not present among you, I want to reaffirm strongly the eminently apostolic role of cloistered nuns. To leave the world to devote oneself in solitude to deeper and constant prayer

is none other than a special way of living and expressing Christ's Paschal Mystery, of revealing it to the world and, therefore, of being an apostle.

It would be an error to consider cloistered nuns creatures separated from their contemporaries, isolated and as if cut off from the world and the Church. Rather, they are present to them, and in a deeper way, in the heart of Christ, as *Lumen Gentium* (no. 46) affirms. It is therefore not surprising that the bishops of the new Churches solicit, as an eminent grace, the possibility of receiving a monastery of contemplative religious, even if workers for the active apostolate are still in such insufficient number.

Sisters of the contemplative life! May your vocation be dear to you; it is more precious than ever in today's world, which seems unable to find peace. The Pope and the Church need you; Christians count on your fidelity.

50. May you who are consecrated to the works of the active apostolate always be more greatly convinced of the Council's teachings, so appropriately recalled in the Code. Live them! That is, may your lives be steeped in the apostolic spirit and may your every apostolic action be inspired by an evangelical spirit.

In this way your activities will constitute an authentic "service," humbly respectful of persons, concerned with avoiding undue pressures and every intolerable overbearing characteristic.

I exhort you again never to forget that the religious apostolate is, by its nature, communitarian: the witness given by a religious cannot be purely individual; it is communitarian in nature, and all religious are called to exercise the apostolate along the line of the charism recognized by the Church and through the mandate of their lawful superiors.

It is not a matter of a simple disciplinary dependence, but of a reality of faith. We must ceaselessly remind ourselves that we are in the Church, intimately incorporated in it, ordained to its mission, inseparable from its life and from its sanctity, as *Lumen Gentium* teaches.

This conception must stimulate in religious the will to work in close and profound union with the Church's Magisterium and its hierarchy. Certainly, in carrying out the multiple, traditional forms of your apostolate, you must not fail to listen to your contemporaries in order to understand well their problems and their difficulties and be better able to help them.

Never forget, however, that the schools, the hospitals, the relief centers, the initiatives directed toward service of the poor, and the cultural and spiritual development of peoples not only preserve their relevance but, appropriately brought up to date, often are revealed as special places for evangelization, witness and authentic human advancement.

51.   Sometimes it may be necessary to abandon works or activities in order to be able to dedicate oneself to others, to create more limited communities in order to answer the most pressing needs of the poor in certain regions. I know your ardent desire to be present to the poor, and I appreciate your efforts in this regard. However, as I said recently to the religious of Sao Paulo (July 3, 1980),[1] it seems opportune to recall here certain exigencies of new forms of presence.

First of all, these efforts must always be conducted in a climate of prayer. The soul which lives constantly in the presence of God and lets itself become permeated with the warmth of his charity will easily escape the temptation of individualism and the contradictions which risk division; it will be able to interpret in the light of the Gospel the option for the poor and for the victims of the selfishness of men, without yielding to socio-political radicalism which, sooner or later, produces effects contrary to those hoped for and engenders new forms of oppression. Finally, the person in touch with God will find the way to come close to people and to become part of their milieux, without losing her own religious identity, and neither hide nor disguise the uniqueness of her vocation which is to follow Christ, poor, chaste and obedient.

Moreover, these experiences must also be prepared for by serious study in a constant dialogue in the heart of the Institute, with responsible superiors and in collaboration with concerned bishops. In this way, the programs will be worked out after examining the possibilities of success (cf. Lk 14:28 ff.), without running risks, but always acting in conformity with the most urgent needs and according to the nature of the Institute.

In conclusion, it will be important always to pursue such experiments in accord with the hierarchy, attempting humbly and courageously, if necessary, to correct them, to set them aside or to adapt them in a more suitable manner.

Above all, always and in everything, behave as loving daughters of the Church, generously and faithfully adhering to its authentic Magisterium, the guarantee of fruitfulness. The fidelity promised to Christ can never be separated from fidelity to the Church: "He who hears you, hears me" (Lk 10:16).

52.   The Holy Year, which we have been celebrating since March 25th, and the preparation for the Synod of Bishops next September are of invaluable assistance to you in carrying out your mission of evangelization.

The Holy Year invites us to rediscover the riches of salvation, and so it calls us to a personal commitment to renewal, through penance and conversion.

The celebration of this event is, for all Christians and therefore for religious, an earnest appeal to repentance and conversion. It makes us rediscover a sense of sin and become aware of the fact that we are sinners. It makes us rediscover a sense of God. This attitude of conversion will especially show itself in a more sincere approach to the sacraments, and it will impel us to practice a charity that is based on truth and that promotes justice. I would like to emphasize at this point the real and profound link that exists between the fraternal life of religious and the very theme of the Holy Year. This is perfectly highlighted by the new Code of Canon Law: "By their fraternal communion, founded and rooted in charity, religious will give an example of universal reconciliation in Christ" (Canon 602).

In this same spirit of communion and joy, I wish to repeat my cordial welcome to all of you who have come to Rome for this meeting. My contact with the members of the two International Unions of Superiors General is a valued way of reaching the religious of the world and of maintaining a continuing contact with the development of religious life. On Tuesday of this week I had the pleasure of meeting with the executive committee of the Union of Men Superiors General. Today I meet with you and I hope to have further contacts with both Unions in the future. When you go home, carry with you my special blessing to the sisters of your Congregations.

53. May the Blessed Virgin Mary, the first of the redeemed, the first to have been closely associated with the work of the Redemption, always be your guide and model. Like Mary, the Mother of Jesus, who was totally consecrated to the Person of her Son and to the service of the Redemption, may you and your sisters learn to know nothing except the Crucified Jesus, who became for us wisdom, justice, sanctification and redemption (cf. 1 Cor 1:30; 2:2).

---

[1] Cf. Book I—nos. 618-647.

7

TO WOMEN RELIGIOUS IN MILAN

May 20, 1983

54.   My visit to this archdiocese on the occasion of the National Eucharistic Congress has a well-defined and significant characteristic: it is a journey of witness, of catechesis and of adoration of the Blessed Sacrament. Therefore, I could not omit a special meeting with you, religious, who are consecrated precisely to Christ, present in the Eucharist, and who have prepared for this great event with intense prayer.

I greet you cordially and express to you my gratitude and esteem for the enormous and careful work carried out by you and by your individual Congregations in the service of this local Church and of the Lombardy region. How many spiritual and also social fruits your love for Christ and for the brethren has produced! An immense array of consecrated souls from century to century has spread everywhere goodness, love, charity, relief, joy, well-being, consolation. Children have been received and educated, parents helped and advised, young people loved and guided, the sick cared for and comforted, the poor helped and consoled, those discriminated against and those gone astray have been lovingly taken in and cared for. Certainly, it has not been possible to relieve every suffering and eliminate all distress; perhaps there have been deficiencies and defects. But it is impossible not to recognize sincerely the immense work carried out in this land with love and with dedication, at times heroic, by the sisters of the various Congregations; by you, who find strength and happiness, serenity and courage in intimate union with the Eucharistic Jesus. Wherever your love and your smiles pass, through the grace of God, good flourishes! For all of this, let us together thank the Lord, who has called you and chosen you for such dignity and given you such a noble and ever authentic mission. And at the same time let us pray that, also through your fervent witness, he give to today's Church numerous and holy vocations, so necessary for modern society, which above all needs love, understanding, mercy and hope.

My greeting therefore becomes a wish and an exhortation to be ever more fervent in the commitment to your sanctification and fraternal charity, and it is extended to all your fellow sisters who could not be present at our meeting because of unbreakable commitments and reasons of health. My greeting goes with special affection to the numerous cloistered nuns who, in continual prayer and self-giving, are an irreplaceable and fruitful part of the Church and of the social organism itself.

55.   The important event of the National Eucharistic Congress which urged me to come as a pilgrim to Lombardy also suggests to me the recommendation I leave you this evening: that your Eucharistic spirituality may always be deeply dogmatic.

The Eucharistic dogma affirms the true, real, substantial presence of Christ who offers himself to the Father as a sacrifice in our name and who is intimately united with us in Communion. The Council of Trent, recalling and interpreting with definitive authority the words spoken by Jesus both in the discourse on the Bread of Life (Jn 6) and at the Last Supper, expressed itself in this way: "The Church of God always had this faith: immediately after the consecration, under the appearance of bread and wine there is the true Body of our Lord and the true Blood, together with his soul and his divinity. His Body exists under the appearance of bread and his Blood under the appearance of wine by virtue of the words of consecration. His Body is also under the appearance of wine, his Blood also under the appearance of bread, and his soul under both appearances by virtue of that connection and natural concomitance which holds united all the parts of Christ the Lord, who rose from the dead never to die again. Finally, the divinity is found present through its admirable hypostatic union with the body and soul of Christ. It is therefore very true that as much is contained under one of the two species as under both. In fact, just as Christ is whole and entire under the appearance of bread and under every part of the same appearance, he is also whole and entire under the appearance of wine and under its parts" (*Sess.* XIII, 3).

Then, interpreting the affirmations of the Apostles, of the Letter to the Hebrews, and of the whole early Church, the Council of Trent affirms and explains that the Eucharist is the "sacrificial presence" of Christ in time, that is, the Eucharist is the renewal of the Sacrifice of the Cross.

The Second Vatican Council reaffirms the same truth: "As often as the Sacrifice of the Cross in which 'Christ our Passover has been sacrificed' (1 Cor 5:7) is celebrated on an altar, the work of our redemption is carried on" (*Lumen Gentium*, 3; cf. *Sacrosanctum Concilium*, 47).

56.　Therefore, nourish your spirituality and your catechesis with dogmatic truths! Read and meditate on the great and fundamental doctrinal documents of the Church regarding the Eucharist, the encyclicals, and statements of qualified and authentic teachers, the experiences of the saints and mystics! There can be no confusion or mystification about the Eucharist!

Saint Thomas Aquinas well said that the truth of the Eucharist "cannot be grasped with the senses, but only with faith, which is based on the authority of God" (*S. Th.* III, 75, 1). And Saint Ambrose, the great Bishop of Milan (334-397), wrote: "Not without significance do you say 'Amen,' since now in your spirit you confess that you receive the Body of Christ. Therefore, when you come up to request it, the priest says to you: 'The Body of Christ,' and you answer: 'Amen,' that is, 'It is true.' One's inner conviction safeguards what the tongue confesses" (*De Sacramentis* IV, 5, 25).

57.　The Christian is convinced that as a creature he must pray to and adore God, the Creator and Lord of the universe and of his life; but enlightened by faith he knows that true "adoration," perfectly valid, worthy of the infinite sanctity of God and of his own personal intelligence, is possible only through the Sacrifice of the Mass, to which every other prayer is linked. One cannot live without adoring and therefore one cannot live without the Mass! The Christian knows that Jesus is present in the form of "food" and "drink," because he "gave himself" totally to man and wants to unite himself intimately with us to strengthen us in faith and will, to console us during tribulations, to transform us into himself, to inflame us with love toward all creatures. Only from the Eucharistic dogma, precisely understood and totally lived, come the true meaning of Christian existence, the strength of the religious vocation, the authentic commitment to the transformation of society, the enlightened sense of unity in Christ, in truth and in charity.

In the same work on the sacraments, Saint Ambrose wrote: "Receive every day what must do you good every day!...And live in such a way as to be worthy to receive it each day! Whoever has been wounded goes to be healed. Our wound is this, that we are under sin, and the medicine is the heavenly and adorable sacrament" (*ibid.,* V, 4, 25).

58.　May the Eucharist, that is, Holy Mass and Holy Communion, truly be the affective and dynamic center of your consecrated life and of each of your communities so that the very virtues of Christ may always shine in you: strength, patience, goodness, generosity, total gift of self, and supernatural joy. Sometimes this all means heroic and enduring sacrifice! But it also means always feeling more need for the Eucharist and a longing for heaven. In *The Way of Perfection,* Saint Teresa of Jesus wrote: "The soul which intensely desires to feed on this food will find in the most Blessed Sacrament spiritual delight and consolation, and as soon as one has begun to taste it there will no longer be trials, persecutions or toils which he cannot bear easily" (c. XXXIV, 2).

59.　Beloved! May the most holy Virgin be close to you and sustain you. As Saint Ambrose exhorts, may she be "the model for your lives" (cf. *De virginibus,* 1, II, 2, 6).

In one of her apparitions to Saint Catherine Labouré, Our Lady said to the young sister, frightened by the greatness and the difficulty of the mission which had been entrusted to her: "It is here at the foot of the tabernacle that you must seek strength and consolation!" The heavenly Mother addresses the same words to each of you. With the Eucharist, near the tabernacle, may you be holy and fearless sisters, today and for the rest of your lives!

With this wish, I impart to you my heartfelt Apostolic Blessing.

8

TO PRIESTS, MEN RELIGIOUS AND
SEMINARIANS IN VENEGONO

May 21, 1983

60.   Evening approaches in man's sky and the day draws
to a close.

But the Lord, heeding the passionate prayer of his
disciples, remains with us to continue life's journey together
with us, to share with us its difficulties, to make us his
heritage forever and to make us "one body."

This is the message, profound and extraordinarily
present, of the Scripture readings we have just heard.

Dear brothers—priests, religious, seminarians—of
the great, ancient, distinguished Diocese of Milan, which
has given to the Church outstanding figures of men of God
such as Saint Ambrose and Saint Charles and some Roman Pontiffs of rare stature!

I am happy to be here with you today, and I address
an affectionate greeting to each and every one individually, beginning with your Archbishop, Cardinal Martini,
and then the person who for many years was your pastor,
Cardinal Colombo. I also greet all the bishops present, as
well as the seminarians from the other dioceses in Italy
who have come in such great numbers.

During this sacred concelebration, beginning with
the liturgical texts proposed to us, I want to pause with you
over a fundamental consideration, namely, that the development of the Christian community is based on the central-
ity of the Eucharist. As a result, the priest, as the minister
par excellence of the Eucharist, the religious because of his
consecration, the seminarian because of his choice directed
towards the goal of the priesthood, if they wish to collaborate in the building up of the People of God, and it is

to this that they are called, cannot but root their entire lives in the Eucharistic mystery.

61.   Above all, the Eucharist, as a memorial and expression of the greatest and truest love borne to men, is the power for renewal of the modern world.

Today, in fact, through various signs and on different levels, the world, which has distorted or lost the sense of sin, is affected by the evil of hatred, which brings with it enmity, division, violence. Hatred can be conquered only with the power of love. And just as hatred appears ancient, so love is always new.

Because it is still extraordinarily relevant, the picture of man in the modern world described by the Second Vatican Council remains vivid in our minds. Even if as never before the human race has at its disposal so much wealth, potential, and economic power, a large portion of humanity is still plagued by hunger and extreme need.

Never before have men had such a keen sense of freedom as they do today, but at the same time new forms of social and psychological slavery are appearing.

Although the world is becoming more vividly aware of its unity, of mutual dependence in a necessary solidarity, it is most grievously torn into opposing camps by conflicting forces. For political, social, economic, racial and ideological antagonisms still persist, and the peril of a war which would annihilate everything remains. (cf. *Gaudium et Spes,* 4).

62.   Dear brothers, a city such as Milan is, in a certain sense, the reflection of the world situation, with its extraordinary resources for good, but at the same time, with its profound and marked contradictions.

And so, this world needs Jesus, his message of love, his Eucharistic presence, which is the source of salvation and unity. Only Christ's mediation can break the spiral of hatred, injustice, violence, sin. Christ is our wealth, our nourishment, our peace, our truth, our freedom. With him, through the transforming energy of his love, man's heart can change, a new being can be born who does not follow the idea of the vindictive teaching of "an eye for an eye, a tooth for a tooth" (Mt 5:38), but the evangelical teaching to consider others as children of a common Father, to love one's enemies, to forgive always without counting the number of times we have forgiven. The water capable of quenching man's thirst springs only from the Word of Christ.

63.   By means of the Eucharist we rediscover the identity of our Christian being. God loves us because he is love. We love because he has loved us first (1 Jn 4:8). Love has decisive importance in Jesus' teaching. But man's love for God is expressed in his love for man. "Everyone who loves has knowledge of God." And "one who has no love for the brother he has seen cannot love the God he has not seen" (1 Jn 4:7, 20).

Thus love for one's neighbor becomes not only the beginning of knowing God, but also the golden rule of love, based on the very measure of Christ's heart. "This is my commandment: love one another as I have loved you" (Jn 15:12).

So, it is the indication of measure.

And Jesus loved us even to the height of service, even to the maximum limit of love with the gift of his very life: that is, without measure.

64.   It was necessary for our salvation that Christ give himself to the Father in sacrifice. Enmity and hatred have been dispelled and destroyed in his flesh with the shedding of his Blood on the Cross, since it is not only the Spirit and water which testify to this, but also blood (cf. 1 Jn 5:6). Thus, Jesus is our sacrificial victim in rendering thanks (Eucharist).

In the Pauline affirmation that we have been chosen and created to be in the Son and to be in the Father's sight (cf. Eph 1:3-5) our faith shows us Jesus, who presents us and offers us. He, the Lamb, remains before God for eternity, with his open wounds, which have become the dwelling of the believers who have become incorporated in him. And the Father considers us in the perspective of the Son who gave himself in sacrifice for us.

65.   Therefore, when we celebrate the Eucharistic mystery, which is the *mysterium fidei* (mystery of faith), we proclaim the Lord's death. By means of the Eucharist, the faithful, marked earlier by Baptism and Confirmation, do not take part in just any meal, but receive what Saint Augustine calls our "mystery," taking what they already are, becoming fully a part of the Body of Christ. This is the proper identity of the Christian being, which does not reside in us but in God.

66.   The Eucharistic sacrament, which is the memorial of love, the bond of charity, is at the same time the sign which produces union and community.

In proclaiming the Lord's death, his Resurrection is prefigured at the same time, since the Eucharistic Body is also the glorious Body. Christ's Body is always the real and personal body which lived, died and is now glorified. In the Eucharist there is renewed the Paschal Mystery, which is the mystery of pain, of death and of resurrection, of Jesus and of mankind. Thus, seen in its totality, the body of flesh, having become the body of glory, unites the faithful to it and among themselves. In this way the Church, a living organism in continual growth, is built up.

It is because of the Eucharist that the members of the Christian community are identified mystically with the Body of Christ, which is the Church, and become one.

Therefore, all the sacraments, as well as all the ecclesiastical ministries and works of the apostolate, are closely bound up with the Holy Eucharist and ordained to it. The Eucharist is truly the heart and the center of the Christian world. In it is contained the Church's entire spiritual wealth, Christ himself, the living Bread, who through his flesh, made vital and vitalizing by the Holy Spirit, offers life to men (*Presbyterorum Ordinis,* 5).

It is not possible to form a Christian community "which does not have its basis and center in the celebration of the Holy Eucharist. Here, therefore, all education in the spirit of community must originate" (*ibid.,* 6).

67.　It is in the light of such reflections, developed on a Scriptural and Conciliar foundation, that we can and must see the Eucharistic mystery as the center and the root of the whole life of the priest, the religious, the seminarian, both from the point of view of personal spirituality and of pastoral mission.

It is in the secret of the Eucharistic source that man, chosen from among other men through God's love, must find his fruitfulness if he wants to remain faithful to his ministry and return richer, in order to give, in the midst of the community of the brethren. To center one's life on the Eucharist means to place at the center of our thoughts and perspectives not ourselves, our human programs, but him, the life of our lives. Otherwise we become withered branches, clanging cymbals.

68.　Dear brothers, so that we may be ever more transformed into the Body of Christ, the Council does not tire of recommending to us the following of Christ as the only thing necessary, the assimilation of his supereminent knowledge, daily conversation with him, and personal and liturgical Eucharistic worship (*Presbyterorum Ordinis,* 18; *Perfectae Caritatis,* 6; *Optatam Totius,* 8).

It is an invitation to walk with conviction along the path of sanctity, since only in this way can we fulfill our mission, which is that of proclaiming and witnessing Christ; only in this way can we give light and consolation to the men of today, whose salvation, as for the men of yesterday and of always, is found solely in the truth made known to us by Divine Revelation.

I trust and hope that this seminary of Venegono, one of the Church's largest, conceived by Cardinal Ferrari and completed by Cardinal Schuster, may be for the Lord's future priests a school of the Eucharist.

May the Virgin Mother, who through the action of the Spirit formed the physical body of the Savior and, as Mother of the Church, accompanied the establishment and development of the Mystical Body, help all priests and seminarians to learn deeply the secret of the life of the Son who became our Brother.

This is a reason for faith and hope for the future of the Church and of the world.

9

TO THE GENERAL CHAPTER OF
THE FRIARS MINOR CONVENTUAL

July 9, 1983

69. I greet you all with sincere affection, members of the General Chapter of the Friars Minor Conventual who, assembled in Assisi, near the venerated tomb of your Seraphic Father, have given to your great Franciscan family the 116th Minister General of the Order in the person of Father Lanfranco Serrini. To him I express my congratulations on his election and above all my most fervent wishes that, following the footsteps of Saint Francis, he may carry out in the best possible way the responsibility to which he has been called, and that he may have good results in the government, or rather in the service, of the more than 5,000 Friars Conventual spread throughout the whole world.

70. I likewise express my appreciation and gratitude to all of you Chapter Fathers for the valuable contribution of suggestions and proposals which you are offering in this important session, with a view to the revision of the Constitutions and of the General Statutes in the context of the new Code of Canon Law, and also with a view to the commitment you have assumed to approve the "Directory of Formation" on which the whole Order, on various levels, has worked over the course of the last two years. I am also pleased to know that among the numerous other goals which brought you together, there is also that of preparing the text of a "Course of Permanent Franciscan Formation" for the religious of the Order, with particular reference to educators.

71.   The deep affection which I have for your Franciscan family—evidenced by my two pilgrimages to the tomb of Saint Francis, respectively the day after my election to the Chair of Peter, and on the occasion of the eighth centenary of the birth of the Saint—moves me to express to you some thoughts inspired in my soul by your presence.

You are Friars Minor Conventual and you want to preserve and to live authentically the charism left to you as a heritage by your inspired Founder. To this end, immersed as you are in a society in continual transformation, it is important to question yourselves on what is essential and irreplaceable in the type of life you have embraced in responding to the Franciscan vocation. It seems to me that one thing which cannot be changed or substituted is above all the *spirit of renunciation,* like that of the Poverello of Assisi. One cannot live your charism fully without accepting discipline with perfect joy, without loving the rule which makes you strong and free, without embracing self-denial, the vigilance over your own thoughts and behavior, and above all without keeping deeply impressed in your heart the words of Christ: "None of you can be my disciple if he does not renounce all his possessions" (Lk 14:33).

72.   The Friar Minor Conventual is a man detached from the greed to possess and therefore does not share the common form of life founded on the search for temporal prosperity: following the example of the Seraphic Father, he flees what the world seeks, searching rather for what the world despises, that is, joyful poverty, interior recollection, a transparent and chaste life, voluntary penance and serene submission to superiors, who are the manifest signs of God's will.

In order to be reliable witnesses to the eternal truths in the midst of this world, the Friar Conventual must make his own the experience of Saint Paul, and for that matter, of all the saints, and repeat with them: "We do not fix our gaze on what is seen but on what is unseen. What is seen is transitory; what is unseen lasts forever" (2 Cor 4:18). The pivots, therefore, on which his whole life must turn are the search for God and prayer, which free man from all earthly conditioning, restoring his true identity to him. To this end, Saint Francis "spent all his time in holy recollection, in order to imprint wisdom in his heart; he was afraid of regressing if he was not always making progress. And if at times visits from the laity or other matters were pressing, he cut them short more than ended them, in order to take refuge again in contemplation. Because to him, who was feeding on heavenly sweetness, the world proved to be tasteless, and the divine delights had given him no appetite for the coarse foods of man" (*2 Celano* LXI, 94; FF I, p. 629).

73.   May this wonderful example be for you a constant incentive to react against certain modern tendencies which, in religious life, would want to put conversation with God in second place, whether it be individual or communitarian, as well as the sacramental and liturgical rites, in order to give a certain preference to other horizontal purposes which, although good in themselves and worthy of being followed, are nevertheless always dependent on the primary end, namely, the spiritual end, which must inspire the whole life and work of the Christian and particularly of the religious.

74.   Another aspect which seems to me to constitute an essential part of the Franciscan charism is total and generous *fidelity to the Church*. It is a question of adhering lovingly and firmly not to an imaginary church, which each one could conceive and structure in his own way, but to the Catholic Church as it is, that is, as Christ willed it and instituted it with its purposes, its laws, its means of salvation and its indispensable structures. What is expected today from the spiritual sons of Saint Francis is that they be able to enliven from within this one true Church of Christ, that they fortify it and enrich it with their complete fidelity, with their absolute obedience: in a word, with all those ascetic virtues which are proper to the Franciscan tradition.

75.   Always have before your eyes the great problems which today occupy and concern the Church: priestly and religious vocations, the missions, the advancement of the lowly, the poor and the weak, the defense of justice and peace; in other words: the proclamation of the "Good News" to everyone of good will. Bring your specific contribution to attaining these great goals. Like your Seraphic Father, be ever more resplendent with the most ardent love for "Holy Mother Church" (XII, FF I, p. 134). In so doing you will reproduce in yourselves his "dear paternal image," you will conform your life to his and you will be true servants of the People of God, capable of lighting everywhere the lamp of hope, of confidence and of optimism, which finds its source in this same Lord.

76.   The Jubilee Year of the Redemption now in progress recalls to mind the specific message of pardon and reconciliation which was entrusted to the sons of Saint Francis with the Portiuncula Indulgence. This is a message of grace and mercy of which you yourselves are the first beneficiaries. Therefore, above all, cherish in this Jubilee the *great pardon* which Francis implored from Christ, through the intercession of the Queen of Angels. In the spirit of the Holy Year, renew in yourselves the humble and joyous invocation of the grace of the reconciling God, and always be more clearly aware of your debt to him, who offered to you, "once for all" (Heb 9:12) and continually makes present to you, with unchanged goodness, a pardon, to which no one has a right, and he pours into you the joy of living your consecrated life in depth. May this fruit of the Indulgence be among the spiritual fruits of your General Chapter.

77.   May the examples of the great Assisian and of all the saints of the Franciscan tradition who have honored the Church assist you. May the shining and courageous figure of Saint Maximilian Maria Kolbe, martyr of charity and exemplary model of Franciscan life for our time, whom I myself had the joy of numbering among the heavenly company of saints, and whose "City of the

Immaculate" I had the joy of revisiting during my recent apostolic pilgrimage to Poland, be of particular comfort to you. As you follow in his footsteps, may the Immaculate Virgin Mary, the Queen of the Franciscan Order, always shine before your eyes and dispose you to an ever more generous dedication to the new and multiple apostolic activities which await you.

May you be sustained also by my prayers for the success of your religious works, above all, those most demanding ones you carry out in Lebanon, Turkey, China and in the mission territories.

May the Apostolic Blessing, invoking abundant heavenly graces, descend upon all of you here present and upon all the members of your Order.

10

TO WOMEN RELIGIOUS IN LOURDES

August 15, 1983

78.   I have just reminded priests of their sublime and demanding ministry of reconciling sinners to God, which completes their Eucharistic ministry. Your vocation is not to administer these sacraments, although you often play an important role in preparing souls to receive them.

I often remind lay people, the baptized, of their prophetic and royal mission to manifest their faith around them, be it in family, social, professional, political, artistic or scientific circles, and to insert evangelical values into these complex human realities. Baptized, you also share in this role, especially if you are dedicated to the active life. In this last instance, you are being told more and more often that you represent enormous vital strength for the Church which counts on you to complete and support the parish ministry of the priests; to fulfill educational, medical and social functions which correspond so closely to ecclesial charity; to accompany the faithful in catechesis or various organizations; for all kinds of missionary work, etc. The choice of apostolate is so vast, and you offer such availability and such competence!

79.   And yet, my dear sisters, this is not what defines you. Your religious life is first of all a life consecrated to God. And I would say that a sign of this consecration is unselfish love. You are primarily for the world *privileged witnesses of this gift of love,* and this is no doubt what God wants most for this world, before any consideration of your "usefulness" to society. And this is what the Church expects from you, for its own witness, before considering your many useful and effective services.

Yes, first of all, the *vocation* which you received and which was tested by your Congregation is a free gift of God's love. Why you, rather than your sister or your friend? Mary was freely chosen by God. And so was Bernadette, to carry her message. Like them, are you sufficiently thankful to the Lord for this tremendous gift?

And your loving response to the Lord must be equally free. By the gift of your life to Christ, as to the Spouse, you show that the Lord deserves to be loved for himself, that the Kingdom of God according to Jesus, with its apparent "folly," warrants the dedication of our life to it, and that the realities of the hereafter are so strong as to make you want to share in them even now.

80. For you who are contemplatives, this aspect is evident: the free choice of your life of prayer and penance stuns, seduces or irritates the world, but never leaves it indifferent, especially today. But, even if you lead an active life, people must also be able to easily recognize the One to whom you consecrated your life.

81. Unselfish love must also inspire the many services and apostolates which you perform in the Church. You want to serve the men and women around you. And many of your Congregations have not hesitated to reach out to the poorest, to those on the fringes of society, to those whose health is most affected, to those neglected by many sectors of society as "unproductive," but whom you love for themselves, thereby witnessing to the fact that human life is always deserving of love and respect because Christ loves it. And it is the same for all those who devote themselves without measure so that the souls of children, young people and adults will freely accept the faith.

In your community life also, you try to live with deep charity among sisters who did not choose each other.

82. *Your religious vows* help you precisely to live this gratuitousness: obedience makes you available to others, poverty makes you unselfish, chastity frees you from possessive relationship.

83.   At the heart of your consecrated life is the Eucharist, received every day and adored in an oratory of your house or close by. It is in this sacrament that your contemplative prayer and your apostolic or charitable action find their nourishment. For, just as the Holy Spirit transforms the offerings at Mass into the Body and Blood of Christ, so must he transform you, to make of you an offering to his glory, a free offering. This gift will be your joy and your primary witness.

84.   Certainly *your activity will be fruitful* in the Church. And even perhaps the most fruitful! But you do not have to seek after this success, even apostolic, at any cost: it will come *in addition.* As in the life of the Virgin Mary. As in the life of Bernadette, for whom to love was enough. Her religious life seemed miserable as far as health was concerned, and useless, when she was at Nevers. And yet! In fact, the witness she left to the world is especially strong, pure and clear.

This is what I wish for you, as I bless you with all my heart, you and the Congregations which you represent. I bless also the sisters who are ill and those who could not come here. Go in the peace and joy of Christ!

11

TO WOMEN RELIGIOUS IN PALESTRINA (ITALY)

August 18, 1983

85. I am sincerely happy that on this, my pastoral pilgrimage to Palestrina, on the occasion of the feast honoring your patron Saint Agapitus, I am able to meet you, even though briefly, religious of the diocese.

I find you here in the cathedral, close to and before Jesus, before him who is the whole reason of your life. Called, indeed, by God to the faithful and constant practice of the evangelical counsels, you are consecrated in a special way to follow Christ who redeemed and sanctified mankind by his obedience even to the death on the Cross (cf. Phil 2:8). Here, close to the Eucharistic Christ, I wish to tell you of my esteem and that of the whole Church, for your *choice of the religious life* which is the basis and foundation of all the multiple and varied activities which, according to the typical charism of each of your Institutes, you carry on day after day for the glory of God and the good of others.

86. The Church looks with admiration on *your presence* because you are a most important and irreplaceable force in the structure of her life and for the very well-being and promotion of civil society. The charity of Christ which impels you (2 Cor 5:14) has truly expanded your minds and hearts in a continuous dedication to others which finds in all your initiatives—inspired by the directives of your Founders and Foundresses—the most valid and genuine expression of that attitude of total availability for your brothers and sisters, loved and served in and for Christ.

Who is able to judge and evaluate, in purely human statistics, the immense good which you accomplish in schools, colleges, churches, hospitals, in charitable and relief work, in parish work, catechesis, in group apostolates?

And let us not forget at this moment the enclosed religious sisters who in silence, detachment, in prayer and penance are, together with you, a luminous witness to the mysterious vitality and fruitfulness of total and unconditional consecration to God in the religious life.

87.   May you always be serenely and joyfully faithful to this *choice of yours,* which is for the Church and for the world a continuous and pressing call to *the primacy of the spiritual.* In such a perspective the "evangelical counsels" assume an emblematic significance by means of which you are not only dead to sin (cf. Rom 6:11) but alive for God alone. Your whole life is placed at the service of God, and this constitutes a special consecration which is deeply rooted in your baptismal consecration and is a fuller expression of it (cf. *Perfectae Caritatis,* 5).

88.   Consecrated to the service of God, you are also *at the service of the Church.* Your attitude of "ministry" should be sustained and animated by constant *prayer,* study and continuous meditation on the *Word of God,* and by mutual *charity.*

My meeting with you comes in the course of the Jubilee Year of the Redemption which I hoped to be a time of grace and salvation for the whole Church; a time in which each of the faithful should feel especially called to a particularly intense effort of penance and renewal. I invite you again in a special way to live and help others to live intensely this year of grace and conversion.

I entrust you, your ideals and your intentions to the Virgin Mary, Mother of the Redeemer and Mother of the Church, that she assist you always and obtain for you the gift of responding to the will of God with the absolute availability of her *"Fiat."*

May my Apostolic Blessing accompany you always.

12

TO THE GENERAL CHAPTER OF AUGUSTINIANS

August 25, 1983

89.   I am very happy to receive you in this special
audience that is reserved for you, the participants in
the General Chapter of the Augustinian Order, which from
your beginning in 1256 is the 174th in a long series of chap-
ters. I greet the Prior General, Father Theodore V. Tack,
who has directed the Order in recent years, his collaborators, you the capitulars, and through you I wish to extend
my thoughts to all your brothers in all of the forty countries that you worthily represent.

The first thought that springs from my heart in this
important moment is that of gratitude to the Lord, the giver
of every grace, who throughout the many centuries and in
the midst of the many adverse winds of history willed to
keep your Order alive and dynamic; your Order which includes a long list of saints and mystics, which has inspired
thinkers and pastors of great talent and universal renown,
and which now counts in its membership 3,400 confreres
of whom 2,570 are priests. You well know the fundamental importance of prayer in general and of thanksgiving in
the life and teaching of Saint Augustine! He who rose so
high in the contemplation of divine truth and descended
so deeply into the abysses of the mysteries of God and man
understood the absolute necessity of prayer that is humble and totally trusting. As sharp as the intelligence of man
may be, mystery always infinitely surpasses it and prayer
then becomes a need of the soul: "It is in prayer that conversion of heart takes place," says the holy bishop, "and
through this conversion the interior gaze is purified" (De
Sermone Domini in Monte, II, 3, 14).

90.   My second thought is an entreaty: you need supernatural light for the deliberations you must carry
on for the good of your Order in future years and also for
the good of the whole Church. In fact, in this chapter the
election of the Prior General and his immediate collaborators takes place, but above all there are decided those activities and initiatives that have the purpose of promoting
the spiritual and apostolic vitality of all the components
of the Order. They are events of fundamental importance
that demand a great sense of responsibility and also a particular gift of farsightedness.

91.   There are three special events that give an even
greater weight to your assembly: the Holy Year of
the Redemption that is now involving the Universal
Church; the 450 years since the arrival in America—and
specifically in Mexico—of the first group of Augustinian
missionaries; and finally, the preparation for the celebration of the 16th centenary of the conversion of Saint
Augustine (386-387). In order to effectively promote the
"spiritual and apostolic vitality" of the Order, the Chapter has set before itself an attentive examination of "continuing formation," which should include in a serious and
methodical manner, the individual and communal levels,
with special theological, pastoral and spiritual courses as
well as communal gatherings of Augustinians, as stated
expressly in your Constitutions (no. 110). This is a question of the highest importance especially today in the
modern world that so rightly demands religious persons
who are doctrinally firm and spiritually well-formed. This
is a necessity not only for you, Augustinians, but also for
the clergy, religious of other Congregations, and laity engaged in the apostolate. It is a question of a "continuing
formation" that is not simply intellectual, necessary as that
is, but of an integral formation that includes the whole
man, intellect, will, and feelings; a formation that can truly
be called "Augustinian," that is always bringing about
renewal whether in the style of communal life of the Order
or in the updating of the religious sciences.

92.   For all these projects you have a great need of prayer: "Pray in hope, pray with faith and love"—wrote our saint—"pray with constancy and patience" (*Ep.* 130, 19). Prayer is as necessary as the grace it obtains. Your Order has as a principal obligation the task of keeping alive and attractive the fascinating quality of Saint Augustine even in modern society: a stupendous and stimulating ideal, because the exact and heartfelt knowledge of his thought and life excites the thirst for God, the attraction of Jesus Christ, the love of wisdom and truth, the need for grace, prayer, virtue, and fraternal charity, and the yearning for the happiness of eternity.

93.   I, too, accompany you with my prayer, because I am convinced that you have a great mission to accomplish in the modern world, that of making felt the love and the mercy of Christ with the same passionate and burning accents of your father and master. "Late have I loved you, O Beauty ever ancient, ever new, late have I loved you!" cried Saint Augustine with quiet grief; but once the truth had been reached, he consecrated himself radically to it and lived for it alone. He bore witness to it, preached it, defended it, sacrificing himself totally for it: "O eternal truth, true love and beloved eternity. You are my God. To you do I sigh day and night!" (*Confessions,* VII, 10, 16); thus he expressed himself in the "Confessions," and the "Soliloquies": "At last I love you alone, I follow only you, I search only for you, I am ready to follow only you because you alone rule justly and therefore I want to be yours. . .Tell me what I must do to be able to see you, with the hope of being able to accomplish all the commands you have given" (*Soliloquies* 1, 5). These should be your sentiments also, in order to be able to realize the task which you have chosen and which has been entrusted to you.

94.   At the threshold of the Chapter I tell you and all the members of the Order with the same intensity of Saint Augustine: "Love Truth totally and with all your heart!"

—Love Truth before everything, manifesting a deep understanding of the modern society in which we live. Today's humanity is full of people who, like Augustine, are searching for the truth, that is, the sense of their own lives, the meaning of history that is always turbulent and unforeseeable, and still more the reason for the universe itself that slips away from the definitive knowledge of science. Remember what the Saint wrote in the *Confessions:* "I have become a great enigma to myself; I asked my soul why it was sad and why it tormented me so, but it could answer me nothing" (IV, 4). How these words sound so real today! Twenty years ago, in the opening talk of the Second Session of the Second Vatican Council, Paul VI said, "A look at the world fills one with sadness because of its many evils: atheism is invading a part of humanity and creating an imbalance of the intellectual, moral, and social order, of which the world has lost the notion. At the same time that the light of the science of things grows, there is spread darkness about the science of God and consequently about the true science of man. As progress wonderfully perfects the instruments that man can use, his heart declines towards emptiness, sadness, and desperation" (*Teachings of Paul VI,* I, 1963, p. 182). Dramatic statements, sadly true! However, there remains still true and ever more stirring the cry of Saint Augustine: "You made us for yourself, O Lord, and our hearts are restless until they rest in you!" (*Confessions,* I, 1).

Out of the striking phenomenon of "secularization" there must arise the phenomenon of the "maturation" of the faith, that is, of personalization by means of inquiry and individual persuasion. Problematic man who is searching and the Christian today who demands clarity and certainty must be understood, loved, and helped.

95.   —Love Truth, then, above all, with the scruple of orthodoxy, eagerly listening to the Master who speaks within, and staying closely united to the Church, the Mother of salvation. "Let Christ be in your heart, so that your heart be never alone or thirsty or have other springs to drink from. So, the Master who teaches is within; it is Christ! If his inspiration and his anointing are not there,

words outside sound in vain" (*In Ep. Jo.* 3, 13). But it is the Church that must guide along the road of Truth. In this regard Saint Augustine is clear and categorical: "In the measure that one loves the Church of Christ, one possesses the Holy Spirit" (*In Jo.* 32, 8). "They do not possess the love of God who are not diligent for the unity of the Church" (*De Baptismo,* III, 16, 21).

Act in such a way as to be and sow always "good grain," so that whoever hears your word and your counsels can feel himself confirmed in Truth, comforted in the love of Christ and the Church, happy to walk towards the heavenly City.

96. —Finally, love Truth by dedicating yourselves carefully to the work of your perfection. The contemplative dimension is the principal one of your Order, even in relation to the active life, in teaching and in charity. Saint Augustine desired an attentive preparation in the sacred sciences, especially in Sacred Scripture, in order to be able to exercise adequately his priestly ministry, and he gave great value to the common life for a fuller perfecting of himself by means of mutual help (cf. *Rule* VIII, 48). Saint Augustine teaches that the apostle must first of all be "one who prays," then a preacher (*De Doctrina Christiana,* IV, 15, 32). In this regard it is necessary to emphasize the need for austerity of life, a certain seriousness, sense of discipline, and a holy courage whether in making demands in the name of Christ and the Church, or in obeying. An Augustinian must particularly remember that he is an instrument and collaborator of the "grace" of God. It seems that in all his works—inexhaustible mines for meditation—Saint Augustine wants to tell us continually that though there is always need for greater understanding, there is even more a need for greater love. "The more you love, the more will you ascend" (*En. in Ps.* 21, 5). Therefore, to love the Truth signifies in the concrete to love sanctity. "When you begin to feel disturbed in yourself," he admonishes us, "waken Christ who sleeps: rouse up your faith and know that he does not abandon you" (*En. in Ps.* 90, 11).

97.   Dear brothers! To bring to a close this pleasant encounter, I want to take up again the teaching of the
holy Doctor and instill in you a tender and profound love
for the Virgin Mary. In his work that treated of virginity
he wrote: "Mary cooperated, through her charity, in the
birth of the faithful in the Church, who are the members
of this Head, but, through her body, she herself is the
mother of the Head." (*De sancta virginitate,* 6). Mary cooperated with her love to give us supernatural life. May she enlighten you and inspire you in these days of intense work:
may she above all protect and comfort the Augustinian
Order on its journey towards him who is the "end of our
desires," whom on the "sabbath with no evening," we shall
see without end, we shall love without boredom, we shall
praise without growing tired. "See what will be at the end
without end. And what other end is ours if not that of the
coming of the Kingdom of God which has no end" (cf. *City
of God,* XXII, 30).

May you be accompanied by the Apostolic Blessing
which I now impart from my heart to you and to all the
Brothers of the Order.

13

TO THE MEMBERS OF THE
THIRTY-THIRD GENERAL CONGREGATION
OF THE JESUITS, IN ROME

September 2, 1983

98. *"I implore you therefore to lead a life worthy of your vocation. . . Do all you can to preserve the unity of the Spirit by the peace that binds you together"* (Eph 4:1,3).

I am happy to find myself in your midst, as you have wished, to concelebrate the Eucharistic Sacrifice and in this way to beg for an outpouring of the Holy Spirit's gifts on the General Congregation that you are opening.

On this occasion, the words of Paul to the Ephesians, that you heard in the first reading, take on a prophetic meaning. And it is with these same words that I address myself to you with heartfelt emotion. Just as the Apostle did, so I too exhort you to conduct yourselves in a manner worthy of the vocation you have received, to preserve attentively the unity of spirit by the peace that binds you together.

In greeting you I greet all the Jesuits of the world, engaged on every frontier in the life of the Church; indeed this is a great family, called by a special vocation to serve the name of Christ, with a total availability for all the concerns of his Kingdom. At this moment, I feel it is present right here, united by the same ideals, by the same calling of the Spirit that Christ pours out again from his breast upon you, as on all the Church: *From his breast shall flow fountains of living water.*

In this spirit of a blending of hearts, in attentiveness to the divine activity, today the General Congregation begins. It is an official action in the life of your religious family, an important moment to live in unity of spirit. This is a unity of *ecclesial spirit* because you are rooted vitally in the Church, one, holy, catholic and apostolic, that you have pledged yourselves to serve with total fidelity, with an awareness that it is a universal sacrament of salvation through the riches of the truth and divine life that it imparts to mankind. A unity of the *Ignatian spirit,* because that special charism, one that makes the Society a privileged instrument of the Church at all levels, is the all-embracing and distinctive element that the Founder himself wanted for your activity and your mission.

99.   And this unity is born out of one faith, one baptism, one Christian and religious vocation, that is its logical and austere flowering. It is nourished by the ontological reality of the Trinity, that is, by the life of the one Father, the one Lord, the one Spirit. And today, we are experiencing that in a special way: *One body, one Spirit, just as you were all called into one and the same hope when you were called.*

Here you have the theological and spiritual roots of today's events. For having offered me the consolation of experiencing them together with you I give you my heartfelt thanks, my very dear brethren.

This General Congregation takes on, then, a special importance by reason of its twofold objective. In the first place, it must provide a successor to the revered Father Arrupe, whom I am delighted to greet here in person and to express to him the gratitude of all for having continued to sustain the Society by his example, by his prayer and by his sufferings.

Your Congregation has, in addition, the task of setting the orientations, of spelling out the guidelines in the years immediately ahead so that there may be an ever better realization, in the special circumstances of the present moment, of the ideal of the Society as it is set forth in the Formula of your Institute: *"To serve as a soldier of God beneath the banner of the Cross. . . and to serve the Lord alone and the Church, his spouse, under the Roman Pontiff, the Vicar of Christ on earth"* (Apostolic Letter, *Exposcit Debitum,* July 21, 1550).

Such a twofold task is certainly weighty; and it is important that you should keep in mind the orientations and recommendations that my revered predecessors,

Paul VI and John Paul I, communicated to you on the occasion of your most recent Congregations, and that I myself expressed to you on the occasion of the meeting of your Provincials in February of last year. They are orientations and recommendations that retain their full weight and that you should have in mind in the work of the Congregation in order to guarantee the happy outcome on which the vitality and development of your Institute depends. Hence the need to call on the Holy Spirit: *Come, Holy Spirit, and fill the hearts of your faithful.*

100. Your General Congregation is an event that is destined also to have some important repercussions in the life of the Church. This is why I take an active interest in it. The Society of Jesus is still the most numerous religious Order; it is spread out to every part of the world; it is engaged, for the glory of God and the sanctification of men and women, even in the most difficult spheres and in key ministries that are of great benefit to the service of the Church. On that account, very many keep their eyes on you, whether they be priests or lay persons, religious men or religious women; and what you do often has some reverberations that you do not suspect.

Thus my predecessors have many times stressed the vast influence that the Society's actions exercise in the Church. In particular, Paul VI, of revered memory, did not hesitate to state that "a very special bond links your Society to the Catholic Church; your fortune, in a certain measure, has an impact on the fortune of the entire Catholic family" (April 21, 1969; cf. *AAS*, 61 [1969], p. 317). If this responsibility weighs on all the members of the Society of Jesus, it weighs today in a special fashion on you who have been chosen as members of this General Congregation. This is why the Pope in this moment is especially close to you in prayer with his best wishes and his fatherly encouragement. And he repeats this, with the words of the Letter to the Ephesians: *"I implore you. . . therefore to lead a life worthy of your vocation. Bear with one another charitably, in complete selflessness, gentleness and patience. . . Do all you can to preserve the unity of the Spirit by the peace that binds you together"* (Eph 4:1-3).

101.   To this end, I am certain that you will keep well in mind the providential nature and the specific purpose of the Society. As I have said, it is engaged in a wide range of difficult ministries. In the course of the meeting with the Provincials in February of last year, I had rapidly sketched out a picture of the activities that you have been called to exercise: involvement in the renewal of Christian life, in the spread of authentic Catholic doctrine, in the education of young people, in the formation of the clergy, in the deepening of research in the sacred sciences and in culture in general, even secular culture, especially in the literary and scientific fields, in missionary evangelization (cf. *AAS,* 74, [1982], pp. 551-565).[1]

For this array of such differing apostolic tasks, in forms that are both traditional as well as new, in response to the needs of the times that have been underlined by the Second Vatican Council, I address once again to you my words of encouragement, with full confidence, *just as you were all called into one and the same hope when you were called.*

The Pope counts on you, he expects so much of you.

102.   On that account, the very special link that the Society maintains with the Pope, who is responsible for the unity of the Church in its entirety, assures the Society itself of effectiveness and certainty when it expends itself, with full availability and complete fidelity, in the struggle on all these fronts of ecclesial action, today as in the days of its origin.

At that moment, your Founder, desirous of dedicating himself totally to the service of Christ the Lord, at the same time as his first companions, under the mysterious guidance of Providence, made his way to Rome in the days of Pope Paul III, in order to place himself completely at his disposition and to accomplish the missions that the Pope would point out to him and in the places that he would determine; you know how Paul III accorded a very willing reception to this proposal, while seeing in it a special sign of divine action.

103. In this perspective, the "fourth vow" takes on a special meaning. It certainly does not tend to put a check on generosity, but only to assure a sphere of activity that is deeper and broader, in the certainty that the deepest and most secret motivation for this religious obedience, of this bond with the Pope, is that of being able to respond in the most incisive way and with a much greater dedication, "immediately, without delay, without any manner of excuse," to the needs of the Church, in apostolic fields both old and new.

While expressing to you my thankfulness for all that the Society has accomplished during more than four centuries of fruitful activity, I am sure that I can continue still in the future to rely on the Society for support in the exercise of my apostolic ministry and to count always on your faithful collaboration for the good of the entire People of God. You know that the Pope is with you and prays for you so that, in constant fidelity to the voice of the Spirit, the Society of Jesus may continue to draw from God's grace the strength and the drive to carry on its vast and varied apostolate.

104. The Church has always considered your Society as a group of religious, prepared spiritually and doctrinally, who are ready to do what is asked of them in the context of the Church's universal mission of evangelization.

The Supreme Pontiffs throughout the centuries have not failed to entrust these missions to you, looking at the most urgent needs of the Church and trusting in your generous availability. To limit myself to the most recent times, I wish to recall the mission that my venerable predecessor Paul VI committed to you on May 7, 1965: "to resist atheism vigorously with united forces," a mission which I urgently repropose to you, for as long as this "tremendous danger that hangs over humanity" continues (*AAS*, 57, [1965], p. 514).

105.   In November 1966, after the Second Vatican Council had just ended, the same Pope asked you to cooperate in that deep renewal which the Church faces in this secularized world. And I myself, in the above-mentioned discourse to your Provincials, confirmed that "the Church today expects the Society to contribute effectively to the implementation of the Second Vatican Council, just as, at the time of Saint Ignatius and also afterwards, it strove with every means to make known and to apply the Council of Trent and to help in a special way the Roman Pontiffs in the exercise of their supreme Magisterium" (*AAS*, 74, [1982], p. 557).[2] To this end I invited you, and today I renew this invitation, to adapt to the different spiritual necessities of the present day "the various forms of the traditional apostolate that even today retain all of their value" and to pay ever greater attention to "the initiatives which the Second Vatican Council especially encouraged," like ecumenism, the deeper study of the relations with non-Christian religions, and the dialogue of the Church with cultures. In this regard, I am acquainted with and approve your commitment to inculturation, so important for evangelization, provided that it is joined to an equal commitment to preserving Catholic doctrine pure and intact.

106.   Speaking of your apostolate, I did not fail at that time to call to your attention the necessity that is at the heart of the evangelizing action of the Church, to promote the justice, connected with world peace, which is an aspiration of all peoples. But this action must be exercised in conformity with your vocation as religious and priests, without confusing the tasks proper to priests with those that are proper to lay people, and without giving in to the "temptation to reduce the mission of the Church to the dimensions of a simply temporal project. . .(to reduce) the salvation of which she is the messenger. . .to material well-being" (*Evangelii Nuntiandi*, 32). This is the magnificent field of apostolate open before you, to work with renewed zeal, faithful to the mandate received from the Pope, un-

der the leadership of the new Superior General, and in close collaboration among yourselves.

The generous realization of this ideal will increase ever more your apostolic thrust; it will help you to overcome the difficulties that in the mysterious plan of Providence are usually connected with the works of the Lord; and it will raise up numerous vocations of generous young men who, listening to the voice of the Holy Spirit, desire also today to consecrate their own lives for an ideal which deserves to be lived and thus to cooperate actively in the divine work of the Redemption of the world.

107.   The Redemption of the world! Indeed, it is here that your General Congregation coincides with the extraordinary Holy Year during which the Church tries to live more intensively the mystery of Redemption. Your vocation consists precisely in seeking to follow Christ, Redeemer of the world, by being his collaborators in the Redemption of the entire world. Consequently you should excel in the service of the Divine King, as stated in the offering that concludes the Contemplation of the Kingdom of Christ in the *Spiritual Exercises* of Saint Ignatius.

My very dear brothers! May this be, for you, the special fruit of the Jubilee Year: a renewed drive in your vocation, that invites you above all to a personal conversion: "Open wide the doors to the Redeemer," to allow yourselves to be penetrated by the love of Christ and by his Spirit, bringing to pass what is said in the petition that Saint Ignatius recommends in the second week of the *Exercises:* "to know the Lord intimately in order to love him and to follow him ever more closely." Intimate knowledge, strong love and the closer following of the Lord are the soul of your vocation. In other words, you ought to be a Society of contemplatives in action who strive in every way to see, to know and to experience Christ, to love him and to make him loved, to serve him in every way and in all things, and to follow him even to the Cross.

108.   On the other hand, one does not know the Lord—
        and you who are masters of the spiritual life teach
that to others—without at the same time placing oneself
with total docility and abandonment under the influence
of the Holy Spirit, whom Christ has poured out over humanity, as a majestic and ever-flowing river. As we have
heard in the Gospel of Saint John, Christ calls us to come
to him and drink: *If anyone thirst, let him come to me and
drink.* This thirst should impel us to enter into intimate
contact with Christ, to contemplate with him the heavenly
Father and thereby to draw strength, light, perseverance,
fidelity in exterior action.

109.   In order to reach this state of contemplation, Saint
        Ignatius demands of you that you be men of prayer,
in order to be teachers of prayer; at the same time he expects you to be men of mortification, in order to be visible
signs of Gospel values. The austerity of a simple and poor
life should be a sign that Christ is your sole treasure. The
renunciation, with joyful fidelity, of ties of family affection
should be a further sign of your universal love which opens
your hearts in purity of spirit to Christ and to the brethren.
Obedience on the grounds of faith should be a sign of your
close imitation of Christ who was obedient even to death
on the Cross. Unity of spirits in a fraternal community life
that overcomes any possible differences or conflicts should
be an example in the Church, in this year when we
celebrate not only the Jubilee of Redemption, but also the
Synod of Reconciliation.

110.   I also ask you that the young men who are recruit-
        ed to your Society be formed from the novitiate
on in this renewed spirit of commitment to exemplary religious life.

        That, my dear brothers, is what the events of today
suggest to us for common reflection. I hope that in this
General Congregation, which is taking place in the Jubilee
Year of Redemption, you may truly follow the voice of the
Holy Spirit that calls you to *do all you can to preserve the
unity of the Spirit by the peace that binds you together.*

Together with this fidelity, may generosity in the service of Christ the Lord and of the Church his Spouse, in union with his Vicar on earth, be the characteristic of every true Jesuit. May it be the impetus of the works of the General Congregation that starts today. May it be the commitment of the government of the new General you are about to elect. All this the Church expects from you. The same expectation is shared by the Pope who participates in this solemn ritual, who unites himself with you in fervent prayer and who blesses you by imploring with you:

Come, Holy Spirit,
fill the hearts of your faithful,
and enkindle in them the fire of your love.

---

[1] Cf. Book II—nos. 260-286.
[2] Cf. Book II—no. 272.

14

TO THE GENERAL CHAPTER OF DOMINICANS

September 5, 1983

111.   On two occasions, according to the primitive chronicle of the Order, Brother Dominic set out from Toulouse, where, with a handful of brothers, he made the *Sacred Preaching* a reality, having begun amid sacrifice and solitude in Prouille, and undertook the difficult and perilous crossing of the Alps in order to reach the Eternal City. He came first in 1215, to request of Pope Innocent III that his little family "could be called, and in reality be, an Order of Preachers" (*Legenda Petri Ferrandi, c.* 27). He was back in December 1216, in order to receive from Pope Honorius III, newly-elected to the Chair of Peter, the Bull of approval of the Order for which he had yearned so much. We know with what veneration and paternal affection he was received by the Popes on each of these two occasions.

I recall these two visits by Dominic de Guzman to the Pope for I, too, wish to associate myself with my two distant and illustrious predecessors in the joy and affection with which I receive you today:

—you, Father Damian Aloysius Byrne, 83rd successor of Saint Dominic, to whom I express the fervent wish that, with the active and generous collaboration of all your brothers, you will be enabled to guide the Order on the apostolic path, in complete fidelity to the powerful and enlightening tradition of those who have gone before you, and with attentiveness to the actual needs of the Church and of the world;

—you, Father Vincent de Couesnongle, to whom I express my deep gratitude and that of the Church for your indefatigable labors during the nine years of your Mastership;

—and you, dear Father Capitulars, who represent the entire Order here, and for whom my wish is one of calm and fruitful work at this time when, like Saint Dominic, you have come here to associate the Bishop of Rome with your reflections on your Order's path.

112.　To you all, I want once more to make clear the attachment which, for many reasons, I have to your Order. Let me even say that, among you, I feel like part of the family. I am sure that the Church, and he who is its universal pastor, can count on your collaboration (as always before) in the arduous task of the evangelization of the world.

　　Indeed, it was with this task in mind that your Order was founded by Saint Dominic. For this, too, your Order was approved and sent out by the Church. Your "mission" still remains the same. My predecessor, Pope Honorius III, writing to Saint Dominic on January 18, 1221, recognized that this mission was inspired by "him who allows his Church to beget ever new offspring." This mission is "to dedicate oneself to the preaching of the Word of God, proclaiming worldwide the name of our Lord, Jesus Christ" (cf. *MOPH*, XXV, p. 144).

113.　"In fact, the Order of Friars Preachers founded by Saint Dominic 'has, from the very beginning, as is known, been specially instituted for preaching and for the salvation of souls.' Which is why our friars, following the mandate of the Founder, 'like men desirous of seeking their own salvation and that of others, should behave honestly and religiously, as Gospel men, in the footsteps of their Savior, speaking either with God or about God among each other and to their neighbor' " (*Constitutio fundamentalis par. II*).

　　"Now, in order to be perfect in the love of God and neighbor by means of this *sequela Christi*, we, bound to our Order by religious profession, consecrate ourselves totally to God and we dedicate ourselves to the Church in a new way, wholly devoted to the preaching of the Word of God in its entirety" (*Constitutio fundamentalis par. III*). To the extent that the Order will be faithful to such needs in the future as it has been in the past, it will be an intimate partner in the universal Church's activity and will be specially close to the Bishop of Rome.

In order to carry out its mission, your Order must hold firm to a number of guiding ideas which arise from the fundamental text I have read to you. These are principles of faith, developed in theology by the great Doctors, among whom Saint Thomas Aquinas shines with particular brilliance. The Church continues to suggest that these principles are foundation stones of Christian wisdom and hinges of the apostolate. It is your role as Capitular Fathers to appreciate the dynamism of these principles in order then to translate this dynamism into regulations or orientations for the spiritual life and work of the Order.

114.   The first of these principles is that which affirms *the absolute primacy of God* in the intelligence, in the heart, in the life of man. You know well how Saint Dominic responded to this requirement of faith in his religious life: "He spoke only with God or of God."

You also know how, on the level of doctrine, Saint Thomas Aquinas, beginning with the Sacred Scriptures and the Fathers of the Church, envisioned this primacy of God and how he supported it with the force and consistency of his metaphysical and theological thought, using the analogy of being which permits the recognition of the worth of the creature, but as dependent on the creative love of God.

And then, on the level of spirituality, Saint Thomas is completely of the school of his father, Dominic, when he defines religious as "those who place themselves totally at the service of God, as if offering a holocaust to God" (*Summa theologiae*, II, II, q. 186, art. 1 and art. 7).

115.   If one does not accept this subordination, if one exalts the greatness of man to the detriment of the primacy of God, one arrives at the failure of the ideologies that postulate the self-sufficiency of man and give rise to the proliferation of errors of which the modern world bears the burden and of which it does not succeed in breaking

the cultural and psychological yoke. The foundations of moral and social life are shaken, whereas, at the religious level, a kind of insensitivity or indifference is frequently manifested in regard to God. One could even speak of the incapacity to face this "struggle with God," which, as the story of Jacob teaches us, expresses in the highest degree the tension of man called to go forward towards a goal that transcends history, where he must live, work, confront trials, and overcome the challenges of time which passes and of death which follows. One could speak of an alienation of man from himself: he loses his dignity and capacity for hope, even when the ideologies would promise him liberation.

116. You, Dominicans, have the mission of proclaiming that our God is alive, that he is the God of life and that in him exists the root of the dignity and the hope of man who is called to life.

You do it as religious by the witness of your lives "totally consecrated as a holocaust to God." You do it as masters and preachers if your theology and your catechesis, like the *kerygma* of the apostles, produces a shock, a break in the closed system where man is on the way to losing himself at the frontier of annihilation. Your proclamation must be addressed to man just as he is constituted by culture, social life, his personality and his conscience, and it must bring him the liberating power of God.

117. Every other study and every other task, in the different domains of the human sciences, economics, social action, etc., are justified if, for you, as religious called to witness and to preach the Kingdom of God, they find their finality and their measure in the higher apostolic goal—taken in its totality—of the Church and of your Order.

Your Constitutions give priority to the ministry of the Word in all its oral and written forms, and the link between the ministry of the Word and that of the sacraments is its crowning.

And from this priority also comes the missionary character of your Order.

In this sense, your Constitutions contain strong exhortations: "In imitation of Saint Dominic, who was full of solicitude for the salvation of each individual and all peoples, may the brothers know that they are sent to all people, believers and non-believers, and especially to the poor. .., to evangelize and establish the Church among non-believing peoples and to instruct and strengthen the faith of the Christian people" (L.I. c. IV, art. 1, no. 98).

The Church today cannot but confirm these laws of yours, bless such projects and encourage your universal missionary commitment, because she knows well that, everywhere, in every place as in each human heart, there is need of God!

118. To this need, this yearning, God has responded throughout history. Through faith we have come to know the work of salvation, which finds its central point, its axis and its fullness in Jesus Christ. And we never slacken in our proclamation of the fact that salvation comes to us through Christ, a proclamation in accordance with the solemn declaration by Peter and the other apostles: "There is no other name under heaven given to men by which we must be saved" (Acts 4:12).

This was precisely Saint Dominic's proclamation, in the footsteps of the apostles. As Saint Catherine of Siena said, Dominic received the "ministry of the Word" (*Dialogue*, 158). In responding to this task, he returned passionate love to the Crucified One. This is marvellously portrayed in Fra Angelico's famous painting: it shows the Saint, pressing his hands onto the Cross, as he embraces, in a look, the form of Christ, so that drops of the Savior's blood run down over him, too. Basing himself on the foundation of the Gospel, Saint Dominic in his preaching insistently proclaimed Jesus Christ.

119. My thoughts turn today to the innumerable brothers, known or not, who during the past 760 years, and even now, dedicate themselves to biblical studies, patristics, systematic theology, either as teachers and preachers, as editors and people otherwise involved in the media, as promoters of the Rosary and as missionaries, in pastoral work and in particular offices of the Holy See.

All of these have but one aim: with all their strength and with generous heart to exercise their ministry as humble servants of the Redemption in today's world.

The Successor of Peter expresses to the Order of Saint Dominic the joyful gratitude of the Church for all it has done until now. And he encourages you today (your General Chapter is, after all, taking place halfway through the 1983 Holy Year) to open up to your brothers, in the tradition of your forefathers, new possibilities of endeavor, both for studies and for the preaching of Christ crucified (cf. 1 Cor 1:23; 2:2).

That which has been taught by the Second Vatican Council on ecclesiastical studies, combined with the indications and guiding principles of my predecessor, Paul VI, on evangelization in the Apostolic Letter *Evangelii Nuntiandi,* and also my own indications in the Encyclical Letter *Redemptor Hominis* and in the Apostolic Letter *Catechesi Tradendae* illustrates a steady plan of work which I earnestly ask your Order to make its own, so that you may be fellow workers in the vanguard of the Church's teaching office and also be prepared to unfold before the world the Kingship of Christ, who died for us and was raised.

120.   We come to the third principle that justifies the existence of a religious Order and orients its activity: *its vital relationship with the Church.* As is indicated in the Code of Canon Law and your own Constitutions (P.I., C.I., no. 21), there is a demand for catholicity, unity and apostolicity if one wishes to be the Church and work on a universal level; one has to make ever more real and visible the fourth mark of the Church, holiness. The link with the Pope is the best guarantee of this ecclesial character; it legitimizes the action of an Order extended throughout the world, guarantees its freedom, and keeps intact its conformity with the norms that regulate the activity of the religious within the local Churches.

Thus I am sure that your Order will never be without its traditional and full obedience to the Successor of Peter, its sincere respect for the Magisterium and that complete fidelity to the Holy See that has always been a characteristic note of your religious family.

121.   My desire for your Order (whose motto is *Truth*) is that you may form numerous sons ready to serve the Church, to work in truth and in obedience, always remembering this beautiful text from your own Constitutions:
"From the moment in which by obedience we unite ourselves to Christ and the Church, every effort and all mortification that we undertake to put this into practice is like a continuation of the self-offering of Christ and acquires a value of sacrifice, as much for us personally as for the Church: in the consummation of this sacrifice is realized all the work of creation" (L.I., art. II, no. 11).
The vital relationship between the Order and the Church has another *essentially theological dimension* that flows from its finality and its nature, which are recognized by the Holy See.
As one reads in your Fundamental Constitution, you are a "clerical Order" in the Church, an Order that has a "priestly and prophetic function" (nos. V, VI).

122.   Your history is proof that there is no opposition between the priestly and the prophetic vocations: rather, both are found together to give to the Order its identity and integrity, just as Saint Dominic desired. It is also true that, owing to the different cultural and religious conditions of peoples and even more, perhaps, to personal attitudes and charisms, one or the other of these functions in particular stands out. In any case, your history, your rule and your doctrine conclude that in teaching, in preaching, in the exercise of the pastoral ministry, the prophetic charism within your Order has received the particular seal of *theology,* understood in the full sense by Saint Thomas as a *wisdom* that bases thought and action on contemplation: this stimulates action, inspires it and rules it (*Summa theologiae* I, q.1, art. 6; II, q. 45, art. 3). Following Saint Dominic, Saint Thomas himself was not only the teacher but also the exemplar of this life of wisdom, toward which it has always been possible for your Order to look as into a mirror of its own "prophetic function," which consists in

"proclaiming everywhere the Gospel of Jesus Christ by word and example," according to the text of your own Fundamental Constitution.

123. On this day I should like to say to you, Capitular Fathers, and to all your brethren in religion: be faithful to this mission of theology and of wisdom in your Order, no matter in what form you are called to exercise it— whether specialized or popular, academic or pastoral, scientific or catechetical. But certainly a place of privilege in the first line of your work (be this work scientific or apostolic) must be accorded to a deepening of the theological and philosophical work of Saint Thomas Aquinas. More so for you than for other Orders, it is necessary to cultivate familiarity with the thought and the writings of this incomparable master and to renew and enrich his teaching.

Your theological function assures the Order of that vital relationship with the ecclesial community from which emerges a variety and richness of charisms which are ordained toward unity by the Spirit, with a view to the building up of the Body of Christ.

124. Lastly, dear Father Capitulars, and still following a path indicated by your Constitutions, I wish to remind you that the secret of a profitable carrying out of your mission in the Church and in the world, the secret, even, of your numerical and qualitative recovery after the crisis which did not spare even your Order in recent years, consists in fidelity to "the apostolic life in the full sense of the word, in which preaching and teaching should overflow from the abundance of contemplation" (*Constitutio fundamentalis,* IV).

It is the fourth principle (but in order of importance the first) on which you will be able to build a present and a future for the Order worthy of its past. It is a principle which becomes concrete in matters you are familiar with and which need only be mentioned here briefly for your reflection and, if deemed necessary, for the resolutions of your Chapter. These are the spirit of prayer, the interior life, zeal, correctness and fidelity in the celebration of the liturgy and, in general, the regular observance of common life, the practice and spirit of the vows, and penance.

Pope Honorius III summed all this up in his letter to Saint Dominic and his first companions when he said that God had "inspired in them the loving desire to embrace poverty and to put regular life into practice" for the sake of the reform of the world and the preaching of the faith (Letter of January 18, 1221, in *MOPH*, XXV, p. 144; cf. *Constitutio fundamentalis*, I).

125. This divine inspiration pointed out the path that must remain yours today. That inspiration has not been modified in any essential way and must not be endangered by structural or functional adaptations or innovations which you have introduced and still do introduce into the organization of the Order in loyalty and in harmony with the Church's directives. Many trial experiments are possible, as long as one does not abandon the correct road. It may even be that, realistically weighing up what has already been tried by way of experiment, it appear to the Chapter that, in relation to some points, a process of re-thinking is necessary.

126. In particular, allow me to suggest that you pay renewed attention to the qualities of conventual life: silence, traditionally seen among you as the "father of the preachers," the habit, "as a distinctive sign of your consecration" (L.1, c. 1, art. V, no. 51); the correct place of the cloister, laid down by your Constitutions "so that...the friars may better attend to contemplation and study, so that the intimacy of the family may grow and so that the temper of our religious life and our fidelity to it may be expressed" (*ibid.*, no. 41). Strengthened by community life, the friars will be enabled to carry out their tasks on the roadways of the world, without hiding their identity, but giving witness to the values of a religious life freely chosen for the sake of the Kingdom of God.

127.	Dear Father Capitulars, how many more things there are which I should wish to share with you with all my heart and as an expression of my affection and appreciation of your Order! May what I say be an encouragement to walk in the steps of your confreres who have marked the history of the Order, indeed one might say, of the Church, with their lives.

Since I must finish, I wish to do so by repeating with you a few sentences from the "Prayer to Blessed Dominic" which was written by his successor Master Jordan and with which you must be quite familiar. I repeat this prayer here as if I were with you before the tomb of your Founder in San Domenico at Bologna, where I have in fact often been.

128.	"You, once you had begun the path of perfection, left all in order to follow, naked, the naked Christ, preferring to store up treasures in heaven. But you renounced your own self with even greater strength, manfully carrying your cross, and you dedicated yourself to following in the footsteps of our only true guide, the Redeemer.

"You, inflamed by divine zeal and supernatural ardor, in the overflowing of your charity and with an immense outpouring of generosity, gave yourself totally to perpetual poverty, to the apostolic life and to the preaching of the Gospel. And to further this great work, and not without divine inspiration, you founded the Order of Friars Preachers...

"You, who so zealously sought the salvation of the human race, come to the aid of the clergy and of the Christian people...

"Be for us truly a 'dominicanus,' an attentive custodian of the Lord's flock" (cf. ed. Scheben, ASOP XVIII [1929] pp. 564-568).

129.	Dear Friars Preachers, I commit you and your entire Order to the care of your holy father Dominic, and I include the entire Dominican family, including, as well as the friars, the cloistered nuns, the sisters of active life, the secular Institutes associated with the Order and the numerous lay people and priests who form part of the fraternities.

And with all my heart I impart to you my Blessing, calling down upon you divine assistance in the work of the Chapter and even more abundant graces for the life of the Order which is so dear to you and to me.

15

TO PRIESTS AND MEN AND WOMEN RELIGIOUS
AT MARIAZELL (AUSTRIA)

September 13, 1983

130.   Mary set out and went straight to a town in the uplands of Judea. The name of the town was *Ain-Karem*. Today *we* set out and have come straight to her, in the uplands of Styria. Here Father Magnus of Saint-Lambrecht built a "cell" in Mary's honor. For more than 800 years she has received pilgrims and has heard their petitions and thanks—here in her sanctuary, "Mariazell."

Pilgrims—with sceptre or staff—have come and are still coming from near and far to commend themselves and their families to the protection and intercession of the "Magna Mater Austriae," the "Mater Gentium Slavorum," the "Magna Hungarorum Domina." Thus they join the great pilgrimage of nations, about which we have just heard in the reading from the Prophet Isaiah: "And nations shall come to your light and kings to the brightness of your rising. Lift up your eyes round about and see: they all gather together, they come to you...and your heart shall thrill and rejoice" (Is 60:3-5).

And again, at this hour Mary's motherly heart rejoices, dear brothers and sisters, as we have come to her as pilgrims at the end of the great *Katholikentag*, to represent, and to commend to her loving care, not only the dioceses of Austria and the neighboring nations, but the entire Church of her Son.

131.   Dear brothers, bishops, priests and deacons, dear members of religious Orders, seminarians and novices, dear brothers and sisters in the lay state! As the People of God on pilgrimage *we are all* "foreknown," "predestined" and "called" by God "to be conformed to the

111

image of his Son" (cf. Rom 8:28-30). The calling we share finds its *particular expression* in the different forms of life and the various ministries in the Church. Still, the Church, as one family, knows no separating barriers between its individual members and groups. All of them are enjoined to rely on each other, to support each other. Thus, each of the meetings I have had during these days was meant for you all, my dear brothers and sisters in the faith in Austria: whatever I said on political and cultural issues, whatever I said to the young and the sick, was also meant for you. And to all of you I address my reflections on the priesthood and monastic life, here before the image of the Mother of God, for your consideration and personal meditation.

132. Today's Gospel culminates with the verse: "Blessed is she who has had faith that the Lord's promise would be fulfilled" (Lk 1:45). With these words the evangelist takes us back from the house of Elizabeth to the room at Nazareth, from the dialogue of the two women to the Word of God. It is God who opens the dialogue with the holy Virgin, with mankind. God is always the first to speak. "In the beginning was the Word" (Jn 1:1). Therefore, dear priests and religious, the first thing we must do in our spiritual life is listen. First we must listen to the Word of God, only then can we respond; first we must listen, only then can we obey. *Silence* and *recollection, reading* and *contemplation* are indispensable elements of our vocation and service as those who listen to and proclaim the Word made flesh. Herein Mary is our example and our help. The Gospels paint Mary as the one who remains silent, who listens in silence. Her silence is the womb of the Word. She keeps everything in her heart and allows it to ripen. As in the Annunciation, listening to God quite naturally turns into a dialogue with God, in which we may talk to him and he listens to us.

133. Therefore, talk to God, *tell him what you have at heart!* Thank him joyously for the mercy he has shown you and for what he gives to others, through you, every day. Lay before him your concern for the people

entrusted to you, children and young people, husbands and wives, the aged and the sick! Lay before him the difficulties and failures you experience in your ministry, lay before him your anxiety and suffering! Dear priests and members of religious orders, *prayer is an indispensable part of our calling.* It is so essential that many other—seemingly more urgent—things may or even must come second to it. Even if your daily lives in the service of man require more work from you than you seem to be able to do, there still must be enough time for silent contemplation and prayer. Prayer and work must never be put asunder. If we go before God every day to reflect on our work and commend it to him, work itself will finally turn into prayer.

134. *Learn how to pray!* Draw above all on the wealth of the Breviary and the Eucharist, which should accompany your daily work more than anything else. In the school of our Lord, learn to pray in such a way that you yourselves become "masters" of prayer and can teach those entrusted to your care how to pray. By teaching people how to pray you will make their—often inarticulate—faith speak again. Through prayer you will lead them back to God and will again give purpose and meaning to their lives.

As I look at you, dear candidates for Holy Orders, dear novices, I am filled with hope. Your seminaries and novitiates should be places of recollection, of prayer, of preparation for an intimate relationship with God. I know how much you want to pray in the right way, and I know that you are looking for new ways to have your lives even more deeply imbued with prayer. Together with you, we all wish to relearn how to pray. Let us be carried away by the prayer of the psalmist: "One thing have I desired of the Lord, that will I seek after: that I may dwell in the house of the Lord all the days of my life, to behold the beauty of the Lord and to contemplate his temple" (Psalm 27:4).

135. Dear brothers and sisters! The Word of God leads us to silence, to our inner selves, to the meeting with him, but it does not separate us from one another. The *Word of God* does not *isolate,* but *unites.* In the silence of the dia-

logue with the Angel, Mary learns of Elizabeth's maternity. From the silence of this dialogue she sets out and goes straight to her in the hill country of Judea. Mary knows what God has done for Elizabeth and she tells her what God has done for herself. To that hour we owe precious prayers: "Blessed art thou among women and blessed is the fruit of thy womb." This is Elizabeth's reply to Mary's greeting, and our daily *Magnificat* is Mary's reply to Elizabeth. Let us remember from the Gospel of today's Mass: God not only calls us, but he helps those who receive his call to understand and accept each other in their different callings.

Jesus wants those he has called to be with him (cf. Mk 3:14), not as isolated individuals, but as a *community.* All the People of God and all the individuals that receive his call are in communion with the Lord and with one another. As in the case of Mary and Elizabeth, this communion embraces both the life of faith and everyday life. This is particularly evident in the case of you religious. You, more than others, live by the example of the ancient Church, when "those who believed were of one heart and one soul" (cf. Acts 4:32). The more you succeed in living together in your communities in true charity, the more convincingly will you bear witness to the credibility of the Christian message. In the words of the Council, "the unity of the brethren is a symbol of the coming of Christ and is a source of great apostolic power" (*Perfectae Caritatis,* 15).

This also holds true for those of you who are diocesan priests and deacons. I know that some of you suffer from *loneliness.* Many of you—due to the growing scarcity of priests—are alone in your work. Perhaps you feel you are not sufficiently understood and accepted in a world that thinks differently and considers you and your message as something strange.

136.   Thus, there is all the more reason for us to take this into account and to strive to live in the concrete what the Council says concerning *priestly community.* Indeed, you secular priests and deacons are never really alone: together you form an intimate community of vocation. For by ordination and mission you are—as the Council states

emphatically—"united together by bonds of intimate brotherhood" (*Lumen Gentium,* 28), and "in an intimate sacramental brotherhood" (*Presbyterorum Ordinis,* 8). You are joined to your "brother priests by a bond of charity, prayer and every kind of cooperation" (*ibid.*). Strive, dear brothers, to live this joyous reality deriving from sacramental ordination in an active priestly community. Together with you, we, the Pope and the bishops, will make this our common concern. Let us do everything in our power, with the help of God, to accept one another as brothers, to share each other's burdens, and thus together to be witnesses of Jesus Christ.

137.   The *celibacy* which you priests and religious *have chosen for the sake of the Kingdom of heaven* makes you freer for communion with Christ and for the service of mankind. Yet it also *makes you freer for closer and deeper communion with each other.* Do not let yourselves be tempted by anyone or anything to diminish or renounce this generous readiness to serve. Rather, bring it to full fruition for your lives and your service for the salvation of man.

138.   Dear candidates for the priesthood in the seminaries, you are full of ideals about your service and the life of priests in our times. With you, let us *open ourselves* to that "which the Spirit says to the communities" (Rev 2:29; 3:6,13,22). At the same time I ask of you: start living your ideals now, particularly the ideal of community—among yourselves and with your superiors—in the life of faith as well as in your studies and leisure time.

The stronger the community spirit in the lives of religious and priests, the more effective their service will be. The way in which they live community will also determine whether or not *more young people* will dare to follow the calling to become a religious or a priest. Wherever convents are full of life, wherever pastoral ministers live together in brotherhood, wherever priests and laity are bound together in the unity of the Body of Christ—it is there that we also find the most vocations!

139.   Dear brothers and sisters, it affords me deep joy and satisfaction to address these words to you in the presence of the holy image of the Blessed Mother of Mariazell. As the Mother of God and Mother of the Church, *Mary is also above all the mother of all those who continue the mission of her Son in history.* In her calling, in her unconditional acceptance of the message of the Angel, and in her praise of God's forgiving mercy in the *Magnificat,* we recognize the mystery and the significance of our own calling. In her faithful acceptance of her election and mission, the Word of God became a historical reality in her. In this way *God's eternal plan* was carried out, about which Saint Paul speaks in today's second reading: "For those whom he foreknew he also predestined to be conformed to the image of his Son, in order that he might be the first-born among many brethren" (Rom 8:29). By her trusting obedience to the word of the Angel, the Virgin Mary *was placed at the center of God's plan of salvation.* By her maternity, the Son of God became a brother to all of us, so that we can conform to his image in justice and glory. For Saint Paul also tells us today: "Those whom God called, he also justified; and those whom he justified he also glorified" (Rom 8:30). The raising of man all the way to his participation in the glory of the Most Holy Trinity takes place through Christ, the Son of God, who became the Son of Man through the faithful *"fiat"* of the Virgin Mary. Indeed, "blessed is she who believed," for behold, henceforth all generations will call her blessed.

140.   Yes, dear brothers and sisters, *we too will be blessed because we have believed, if, like Mary, we set out* from our own personal encounter with God *to proclaim today* to the inhabitants of the mountains and valleys of all countries and continents *the marvels God has performed—in Mary's womb, in Christ, her Son, and in us, his brothers.* For as the Prophet Isaiah tells us in the first reading, "Darkness shall cover the earth and thick darkness the peoples, but the Lord will arise upon you, and his glory will be seen upon you" (Is 60:2). Through the faith of the Blessed Virgin, God's light began to shine and illuminate the new

Jerusalem. It is the shining of the glory of the Most High, of that light which from the beginning illuminates every man, but which seeks to shine its full radiant splendor on everyone in Jesus Christ. This is why we are commissioned to proclaim: "Arise, shine; for your light has come, and the glory of the Lord has risen upon you" (Is 60:1).

141. *Whoever has a spiritual vocation is called to this mission of the Church in a special way.* Christ called his followers to himself, and he sent them out among the people, far from his reassuring presence (cf. Mk 3:14). "Go into all the world and proclaim the Gospel to the whole creation" (Mk 16:15). In this connection I should particularly like to mention all of you priests, brothers and sisters in the missions, who, together with the volunteers delegated by the Church to work for development, proclaim the Good News throughout the world in word and in social action. Whoever you are and wherever you work, your spiritual task is always the same, i.e., to shine with the "radiant light from above" on all who "sit in the darkness and shadow of death" (cf. *Benedictus*). This is your mission, whether you are priests in a city parish or have charge of a small rural community, whether you are religious working in a school or caring for the sick and the poor, or whether you are limited by sickness or old age to a life of seeming inactivity.

142. Indeed, it is you *sick and elderly priests and religious* to whom I feel particularly attached in this hour—I shall even have the opportunity afterwards to greet some of you personally. The entire Church throughout the world commends itself to your concern and your prayer. For your mission there are no longer any boundaries of space. Your language is prayer and suffering, accepted always with renewed courage. To you also the Lord entrusts ever new missions. Your special service—prayer and suffering—is an irreplaceable part of the mission of the Church. At the end of his life the Lord, too, no longer preached. Rather, he took up his Cross and carried it and endured it, until finally everything was finished.

117

143. Dear brothers and sisters who are already priests and religious, and all of you who are preparing yourselves for this spiritual vocation, the Lord has chosen you, so that you may be with him in prayer and recollection, so that you may live out your calling in community, and so that you carry his salvation to the people. At the end of the celebration of the Eucharist, I shall ask the Blessed Mother of Mariazell for her motherly protection and support for this, your mission.

To summarize what I would like you to take with you from our common pilgrimage, what Mary herself would like to give you—and me—from this shrine of hers, to accompany us on our way, I have chosen a phrase that she herself often prayed in her life, a verse from today's responsorial psalm. With it I would once again like to recall the main theme of the *Katholikentag* and ask the Virgin Mary to plant it in the heart of each and every one of you:

"Hope in the Lord, be strong!
Have steadfast courage and hope in the Lord!"
Amen.

16

TO THE ASSEMBLY OF THE UNION OF THE EUROPEAN CONFERENCES OF MAJOR SUPERIORS, IN ROME

November 17, 1983

144.　I am very happy to receive you. This is the first official meeting of the Pope with the representatives—men and women—of the Conference of Major Religious Superiors of Europe, which is still in its initial stages.

Here we are gathered together at the moment when the Church is preparing to celebrate the feast of Christ, King of the Universe, the light that shines at the end of men's path, he who alone is able to bring all peoples the benefits of unity and of peace. Your coming together has as its precise goal to help the religious of Europe to bear witness to the Gospel, more intensely and in a manner ever more adapted to people's needs, in order to establish the Kingdom of Christ.

And how could you fail to be stimulated by the experience of the past? Your predecessors, the European religious, truly accomplished a work of evangelization in every sense of the term. Not only did they win over their brothers of immediate geographical proximity, but they carried the Gospel and the message of Christ into numerous regions which became, thanks to them, authentic lands of Christianity, spiritually rich and fruitful.

You are located in the privileged situation of the European continent, with perceptible differences according to its various regions. Despite the present decline of vocations in many countries, the traditional role of religious creates for them today serious and grave obligations in the area of evangelization.

145. Your vocation itself is for you, religious men and women, a privileged means of evangelization; you witness to the holiness of the Church by incarnating her profound longing to give herself over to the radicalism of the Beatitudes. By your life, you are signs of a total self-surrender to God, for the Church, for the brethren (cf. Apostolic Exhortation *Evangelii Nuntiandi,* 69). The first means of evangelization for religious is to conform their lives more and more to the person and to the message of Jesus Christ. Before any proclamation of the Word, *it is their life itself that should reveal Jesus Christ and his Gospel.*

146. At certain moments of their life, and even constantly in the case of contemplative Institutes, this witness will be the only form of evangelization—a very fruitful one as well, as is revealed by the case of Saint Theresa of the Child Jesus, who in her Carmelite monastery became Patroness of the Missions, and as is likewise attested by the numerous religious, unknown during their lifetime, whose prayer and sacrifices, often continuing right up till their death, have been in all truth an admirable witness to the fecundity of the Gospel, and the seed of Christians. It suffices to mention here the case of Saint Maximilian Kolbe and that of Blessed Maria Gabriella, the Trappistine and apostle of unity! It was in this sense that I spoke to the religious at Lourdes of the gratuitousness of love.

147. The primordial role of *your meeting* should be to assist the religious of Europe to realize better their evangelical mission by living their own vocation more fully. Your national conferences and all the religious have a right to expect assistance, encouragement and collegial support from their brothers and sisters of other nations, in order to confront the problems that transcend national frontiers and affect the religious life of the continent. In this way you will be in a better position to implement an effective collaboration between the national conferences of religious. This action should be accomplished of course with due respect for the legitimate autonomy of these national

120

conferences and Institutes, as also for the legitimate diversities of cultures, of customs, of lifestyles and without any reference to political considerations. Above all, it should contribute to the development and to *the affirmation of the proper character of the religious life.*

148.   Indeed, that which differentiates the members of the Church from one another constitutes a reciprocal complementarity and is ordered to the unique communion and to the mission that belongs to the whole body. Care must then be taken that the religious life preserve its proper characteristics and its visibility. If the Church requires visibility in order to give witness, so does religious life. The attenuation to the point of virtual disappearance to the eyes of the world of that which characterizes the religious life is not good for the religious, or for the Church, or for evangelization. This respect for the specific riches of the religious life should take account of the particular nature of the Institutes such as it had been recognized by the Church at the time of their official approval.

149.   The fact that several countries of Europe are experiencing an increased dechristianization, with baptized persons living practically outside the Church, poses more acutely for Christians and for religious the question of their witness and of their apostolate. Certainly the reasons are complex and stem in part from difficulties external to the Church. But one may ask oneself: have these Christians had sufficient evangelizers, and has the witness of these evangelizers, like that of European religious, been sufficiently authentic and visible? More than all others, the religious should take care not to allow the "salt" of the Gospel to become insipid through secularizing practices and attitudes, sacrificing prayer to an all-too-human pattern of activity, adopting socio-political behavior determined by criteria that are not always evangelical. I know well that you are convinced of this; is it not one of the aspects of spiritual renewal that you are seeking by a revision of your Constitutions?

150.   The authentic evangelical witness of religious concerns also, every day, a more significant number of
non-Christian immigrants from other continents seeking
more favorable living conditions in Europe. It is of the
highest importance that these poor people find in religious
a reflection of the charity of Christ. This is a new way of
continuing what the missionaries of preceding generations
accomplished in distant lands.

151.   This *fraternal charity* ought to be lived first of all
among the religious themselves. Canon 602 sees in
the "fraternal union of the members, rooted in and based
on charity, an example of universal reconciliation in
Christ," a theme developed by the recent Synod of Bishops.
If union within the religious family is a powerful evangelical witness, division among brothers, among sisters, is a
stumbling block for evangelization. Now disunion is not
only to be found among the different Christian communities in Europe, it is also encountered among the faithful
of the Catholic Church. and sometimes even in religious
houses, where polarizations constitute a by no means
negligible obstacle to the witness of fraternal charity.

152.   Moreover, these divisions derive most often from a
practical forgetfulness of the ecclesial nature of evangelization; the latter must always be carried out in the
name of the Church, in communion with its pastors and
not according to individualist criteria and perspectives
(cf. *Evangelii Nuntiandi,* 60). Fraternal union lived in fidelity to the Magisterium will contribute to implanting
the Church, which cannot exist without the driving force
which is the sacramental life culminating in the Eucharist
(cf. *ibid.,* 28).
   Yes, it is in the perspective of the Church's mission,
confronted with its most urgent needs, such as the responsible pastors see them, that the multiple apostolic services
of which your Institutes are capable must be viewed. For
the Church counts on you, she needs you and she knows
that she finds in you, in your Institutes, immense and

marvellous resources for the various forms of its *direct and indirect proclamation of the Gospel.*

153.   At the present time, the Gospel must be proclaimed to a world which is suffering from hunger and privation. Despite discernible differences between the regions, the European continent remains privileged on the economic level; it must not happen that religious, allowing themselves to be won over by the pursuit of comfort and the selfishness of many people around them, close their eyes to the underprivileged categories of society and to the regions of the world that are plunged in misery. They must by their availability and their disinterestedness *come to the aid of the deprived* of every sort. But I will not press the point, because I know to what extent many Institutes, many religious—both men and women—are making an effort today to live poorly and among the new poor that our society hides away. On the other hand, this form of witness does not prevent the undertaking of true responsibilities that are a service. Indeed, *the educational and social action of the Institutes,* according to their proper charism recognized by the Church and in organic collaboration with the laity, always remains relevant, especially if the religious preserve in this area a concern for the poor, for those on the fringe of society, for the immigrants, refugees, etc. Their activity in this direction is more than ever a necessity for evangelization, being a visible manifestation of the love of God for mankind.

154.   The larger view your Union affords of the world, the fruitful relationships it establishes with the Council of European Episcopal Conferences, should enable it to help the national conferences of religious and the various Institutes to offer an ever more effective evangelical witness by *impregnating the different cultures* with the Good News brought by Jesus Christ, without being enslaved by any one of them.

On the morning of Pentecost, the Virgin Mary, Mother of the Church, was present in prayer at the beginnings of the evangelization that took place under the inspiration of the Holy Spirit. May she ever remain the Star that guides religious in their mission and renders them generous and joyously faithful to the Gospel and to the Church!

Confident that your meeting here will be effective in helping the religious of the European continent to be ever more credible witnesses to the Gospel, I bless you with all my heart.

17

TO MEN AND WOMEN RELIGIOUS GATHERED IN ROME FOR THE JUBILEE OF THE REDEMPTION

February 2, 1984

155.   *"Lumen ad revelationem gentium, et gloriam plebis tuae Israel"* ("A revealing light to the Gentiles, and the glory of your people Israel") (Lk 2:32).

Today, dear brothers and sisters, I want to borrow these words of the old man Simeon in order together with you to adore the Light: *Christ the Light of the World!*

We are meeting in Saint Peter's Basilica in the Year of the Redemption, in the year of the extraordinary Jubilee. We are meeting in that great and multiform community which you all make up, brothers and sisters from so many religious Orders, Congregations and Institutes. *Individuals and communities consecrated to God!*

This meeting brings together the representatives of the religious families who live in Rome and, at the same time, extends to all those fellow *brothers and sisters* with whom the *unity and the identity of your vocation* unites you. And through this unity and identity you are bound also by a *special union of mission* in the Church, a mission in the midst of the People of God in every country and on every continent, to the ends of the earth.

Today, in this great universal community, you join the *Bishop of Rome* and the Successor of Peter to cry out in the spirit of today's Liturgy:

"A revealing light to the Gentiles!" The light: Christ the *Light* and *glory* of the People of God throughout the world!

156.   With this cry you want to respond to the spirit of the liturgy of this special feast, and at the same time you want to express what constitutes the interior mystery of

each and every one of you. In fact, *because of your vocation* you walk in a special way in this Light which is Christ, and, in addition, you bear witness to it in a special way.

Today it is manifested by the *lighted candles* which in a short time you will hold in your hands. Each of these recalls above all the *Sacrament of Baptism,* through which Christ began to illuminate your life with the light of the Gospel and with the light of the Redemption: Christ received *through faith into the community of the Church.* Christ passed down from day to day in the life of your Christian family, surroundings and school. The full flowering of Baptism is the *Eucharist;* and, at the same time, the constant renewal of its purifying power is the *Sacrament of Penance and Reconciliation.*

157.   Then, each of these candles reminds you—against the background of the liturgy of today's feast—of *the moment of your consecration:* religious *profession*, the choice of the way of life according to the evangelical counsels of poverty, chastity and obedience.

The light of Christ shone then with *an especially brilliant flame.* The flame of faith and hope joined the vivid flame of charity *concentrated* on the Heart of the Divine Spouse and, at the same time, opened widely through this concentration.

Just so, this Divine Heart is opened widely in the mystery of the Redemption, which we know is universal, embracing everyone and everything.

Depth and universality—these are the two characteristics of the religious vocation which attest to its being rooted in the mystery of the Redemption, in the light of Christ.

Today, the liturgy of the Feast of the Presentation of the Lord leads you toward this light.

158.   So, *you enter the temple,* just as Mary and Joseph once did, who took Jesus to Jerusalem to offer him to the Lord (cf. Lk 2:22). The law of the Old Testament provided that every first-born son be consecrated to the Lord

(cf. Lk 2:23), and this consecration was accompanied by a sacrifice of a pair of turtledoves or two young pigeons.

Today, beloved brothers and sisters, you enter this temple to renew—in the light of the Presentation of Christ—*your offering to God in Jesus Christ:* your consecration to be his exclusive property.

159. From the depths of the mystery of consecration springs this particular *belonging to God himself:* a belonging of which only the person, the knowing and free subject is capable. This belonging has *the nature of a gift.* It responds to a gift and at the same time expresses the gift.

In the light of Christ each one of you perceives, with penetrating clearness, that all of *creation* is a *gift* and you perceive in creation the special *gift* of your own humanity, and with the gift of this entire and indivisible humanity you desire to *respond to the gift* of the Creator, of the Redeemer, of the Spouse.

In this way, there is inscribed in the human "I" of each one of you a special *bond of communion with Christ* and, in him, with the Most Holy Trinity: with the Father, with the Son and with the Holy Spirit.

160. Entering the temple, then, along with Mary and Joseph—where the rite of the Presentation of Jesus provided for by the law will take place—*we encounter two persons* wholly consecrated to God, dedicated to the expectation of Israel, or rather, to mankind's greatest hope of all times: *they are Simeon and Anna.*

Simeon, inspired by the Holy Spirit, had gone to the temple (cf. Lk 2:27).

Does this not perhaps bring to mind *a similar "inspiration"* with which you were once moved: the inspiration of the Spirit? Yes! Since the *Holy Spirit,* in the power of Christ's Redemption, is the *author* of all sanctity. He is also author of that special *call on the way to sanctity* which is contained in the religious vocation.

161. Today, when you renew your profession in your hearts, remember that interior "inspiration" of the Spirit which was at the beginning of your path. Remember how this "*inspiration*" came, how it became stronger, how, perhaps, it returned again after a certain amount of time, until you recognized in it the clear voice of God and the power of the nuptial love of the Lord who was calling you.

Remember this today, *in order to give thanks* with a renewed heart, to profess "the marvels of God" (Acts 2:11). This inspiration "from the Spirit" *cannot be extinguished.* It must endure and mature, along with the religious vocation, during your entire lives.

162. You can never separate yourselves from the salvific "inspiration from the Spirit," caring for it in that *interior temple* which each of you is!

How eloquent are the words concerning the prophetess Anna in today's Gospel: "*She was constantly in the temple,* worshiping day and night in fasting and prayer. Coming on the scene at this moment, she gave thanks to God and talked about the child to all who looked forward to the deliverance of Jerusalem" (Lk 2:37-38). Simeon leans over the child and utters the prophetic words: "This child is destined to be the downfall and the rise of many in Israel, a sign that will be opposed so that the thoughts of many hearts may be laid bare" (Lk 2:34). He addresses these words to *Mary,* his Mother.

And he adds: "And you yourself shall be pierced with a sword" (Lk 2:35).

A strange prophecy! It is perhaps the most concise and at the same time *the most complete synthesis of all Christology and of all soteriology.*

Dear brothers and sisters!

May this prophecy reach your souls today with new strength.

163. *Welcome Christ,* who is the light of the world: Christ in whom God "has prepared salvation in the presence of all peoples" (cf. Lk 2:31).

Welcome Christ, who is also a "sign of opposition." This "opposition" is inscribed in your vocation. Do not try to remove it or to erase it. This *opposition" has salvific significance.* The salvation of the world is achieved precisely along the path of this opposition offered by Christ. You too, by welcoming Christ, are a manifestation of this salvific opposition. It cannot be otherwise. Precisely *in the name of this salvific opposition* there is inscribed in your Christian and religious "I" the profession of poverty, chastity and obedience.

164. The world needs the authentic "opposition " of religious consecration as a constant *leaven of salvific renewal.*

You will carry in your hands *the lighted candles* of today's liturgy.

They say that Christ *is the light* which enlightens every man who comes into this world.

They are the *testimony* of your indivisible dedication to Christ and to God; they are the testimony of your consecration.

These candles also *illuminate human life,* the life of each one of us. As the candle gradually burns, the wax melts and the candle is consumed.

May your lives be consumed in the light of Christ!

May yours be lives of total nuptial dedication to his service!

May the life-giving current of the mystery of the Redemption pass through this life, reaching the world and man and directing all our human existence *towards the eternal light: the light of vision and glory.*

165. Simeon *said to Mary, Mother of Jesus:*

"And you yourself shall be pierced with a sword!"
Dear brothers and sisters!
Receive Christ *from the hands of Mary!*

May the mystery of the Redemption reach you through her soul!

May all the salvific plans of consecrated hearts always be *manifest before the heart of the Mother*! United with her. With your glance focused on her. In her there is a special resemblance to Christ, the Spouse of your souls.

18

TO PRIESTS AND MEN AND WOMEN
RELIGIOUS IN BARI (ITALY)

February 26, 1984

166. *"Os nostrum patet ad vos..."* ("We have spoken to
you frankly") (2 Cor 6:11).

My mouth, or rather my heart, is open in complete
outpouring to you, beloved brother priests and dearest consecrated sisters, in this meeting which the Lord has granted
us to have. I express to you my total joy in being able to
converse with you, and I am grateful for your very affectionate welcome.

I would like to greet you one by one, individually.
On behalf of all of you I also greet your Archbishop, Msgr.
Mariano Magrassi, to whom I express my deepest appreciation. I have come to tell you that I am following you, that
I am accompanying you, that I am happy with what you
are doing in this beloved land of Apulia in the service of
the Gospel and the Church. I know that you are working
zealously and wisely. I know that you spare no effort to
bring the "happy announcement" of the Lord Jesus everywhere. Let us together offer fervent praise to our God, the
source of every good, who has willed to call us to serve him
more closely, that he may guide us on our way, strengthen
our weakness, bring our resolutions to fulfillment.

167. "He who has begun the good work in you will carry
it through to completion" (Phil 1:6). It is with this
certainty that today you—and I am addressing the priests
in particular—intend to renew your response to the Lord
with a new "yes" that is more mature and more authentic.

Our time appears fraught with peril, it knows worri-
some threats and tensions, but it is also very rich in fer-
ments open to good and laden with good promises. This

society, in such rapid evolution and often surprising to us with such erratic attitudes, is a society that paradoxically *yearns for God and is seeking him.*

168.   Respond to this yearning by proclaiming the Lord, speaking about him, communicating him and him alone! In a world that is closed and opaque, reveal the Lord of light. To a society that is lost, manifest the God of hope. To those who deny life, make the Lord of life present.

How will this witness be possible without a profound *spirit of faith?* You know this and experience it every day: the people who are entrusted to you seek you in order to have firm certainties, words that do not fade, absolute values. It is God who is the only certainty, it is he who is the Absolute: that God who revealed himself in Jesus and who, in the death and Resurrection of his Son, has called us to new life.

In Jesus we believe, to him alone do we entrust our life, him we wish to proclaim to the world, to every man and woman. Jesus Christ, who is the Way, the Truth and the Life (Jn 14:6) and is the theme of our thinking, the topic of our speaking, the reason for our living. He is the object of our increasing love; he will one day be our eternal reward; it is from him that every undertaking must draw strength.

169.   This faith, dearly beloved, I ask you to defend, to nourish, to strengthen every day. You are the "professionals" of faith, God's specialists. Know the greatness of this mission, let yourselves be completely caught up in this whirlwind at whose center God himself is at work. Be fully aware of carrying out a mission that cannot be replaced. May the snares of doubt not infiltrate your spirit. Do not let tiredness or disappointment dull that freshness of self-giving that the priestly vocation demands.

170.   May yours be a strong and vigorous faith, nourished by *persevering prayer.* Be models of prayer, become masters of prayer. How necessary it is that your days be marked by rhythmic times of prayer during which, after

the example of Christ, you are immersed in lively and refreshing conversation with the Father and encounter the ineffable God! This fidelity is not easy, especially today when life's pace is frantic and activities are so greatly absorbing. But we must be convinced that the time for prayer is the time when the union of the priest with his people is stronger, when he is more "present" and effective in his ministry.

171. With the universal Church we are living a time of extraordinary grace, which the Jubilee Year of the Redemption is. You find yourselves personally committed. How many times has there resounded from your lips the saying already uttered by the Apostle: "We implore you, in Christ's name: be reconciled to God!" (2 Cor 5:20). And how can you not have felt addressed to yourselves in the first place the urgent call to continual conversion, to interior renewal?

In the Bull of Indiction of the Jubilee Year I wrote that "surely there is no spiritual renewal that does not pass through penance and conversion, both as the interior and permanent attitude of the believer. . .and also as the means of obtaining God's forgiveness through the Sacrament of Penance" (*Aperite Portas,* 4).

172. Permit me, therefore, dear brothers, to call upon you to give ever more value to the Sacrament of Reconciliation. In this, you will be doing no more than following the timely directions of the recent Synod of Bishops. You are in a singular way the beneficiaries and the ministers of the Sacrament of Penance. Who does not see that the priest, constituted by God as the minister of Christ's reconciliation, is called to experience firsthand within himself the gift of reconciliation by making it operative in his own life? We are convinced that it is impossible to offer others the message of reconciliation if we are not capable of living its saving power in ourselves.

In a Church that is called to be renewed, you must lead your brothers and sisters by your example and your life. And by giving the Sacrament of Penance increased value for yourselves personally as a masterly way of purification and growth in the faith, you will gain a deeper appreciation for the immeasurable gift that the Lord has given you in choosing you, his priests, to forgive sins in his name.

173.   Seeing you assembled in this cathedral, in which many of you received priestly ordination, and reading on your faces the joy of being together, I recall the words that Saint Ignatius of Antioch wrote to the Christians in Ephesus: "Your college of presbyters, justly famous and worthy of God, is as closely united to the bishop as the strings of a zither. For this reason, by your accord and the harmonious charity which you demonstrate, a hymn is offered to Jesus Christ. And you, one by one, become a chorus, so that, harmonious in accord and taking the pitch from God, you sing in unison through Jesus Christ to the Father that he may hear you" (*Eph* IV).

174.   What a warning all these words are for us! And what a response they offer for this world that is so divided and selfish! To be and to be perceived as the Church, to increase the communion of the bishop with his presbyterate, to make more evident the communion of priests among themselves, to show that it is possible to meet one another, to love one another, to help one another to the point of sharing goods, finally to conquer the terrible snare of individualism: is this not, brothers, a marvellous program? Would it not be at the same time the most effective evangelization?

I have come to encourage you in your commitment and to exhort you not to let yourselves be depressed by difficulties. Christ, to whom you have consecrated your life, is with you!

175.   And now a word of affectionate greeting, of satisfaction and good wishes to the sisters gathered here. What a joy it is to meet with you! And what hope is stirred up in my heart by your presence, which makes so evident the work of God and the wonderful action of the Spirit!

Know that your witness is important, is valid, is fruitful, is necessary. Your life is marked by the constant search for God: you are women of the Absolute. You seek

Christ with an undivided heart; you bear witness to the world that the Lord is truly worthy to be loved above all things and followed with total dedication. You live for God alone.

176.   But—and this is a truth that is ever surprising—in living for God alone, you do not estrange yourselves from society. On the contrary, in the Lord Jesus you encounter all mankind and go out to it with the strength that comes from him. You intend to be very attentive to the needs of today's man, and as women who have experienced the love of God, you wish to have your brothers and sisters share in that inestimable gift that you have received. So much so that no commitment must appear too great for you and no sacrifice excessively difficult.

177.   I am here to recommend that you believe very strongly in your vocation. Love your consecration with your whole being. I ask you to reaffirm God in today's society, to proclaim the Lord's preeminence over every reality, to attest with your life faith in the supreme and eternal values, to help man discover his dignity and responsibility, to manifest the full relevance of the Beatitudes. And do all of this in simplicity, in humility, in the indestructible joy of a life that is given.

178.   These, brothers and sisters, are some of the thoughts that crowd my mind in this moment of intimacy with you.

Let us entrust everything to the benevolent Providence of God. Let us pray with confidence to the Virgin Mary, the Queen of Apostles, that she may watch over this region, protect this archdiocese, and bless everyone's good resolutions.

To you who are present, and to those who are united with us in spirit, I heartily impart my Apostolic Blessing.

19

TO THE PROVINCIAL MINISTERS OF
THE CAPUCHINS OF ITALY, IN ROME

March 1, 1984

179. I greet in you, Provincial Ministers and Provincial Councillors of Italy, all your Italian confreres and the well-deserving Order of Friars Minor Capuchin.

Your presence here today manifests first of all *a clear desire to demonstrate your fidelity to the Vicar of Christ*, as your Seraphic Father wanted: to be "always subject and submissive at the feet of Holy Mother Church" (*Rule*, Ch. 12). And it also responds to the filial desire to receive *a word of encouragement* for the difficult task of today's "ongoing formation."

180. I know that in recent times your Order has seriously tried to face the treatment of this problem. Clear proof of this is, on a legislative level, the present laws in your Constitutions of 1982 (*ibid.*, nos. 41-44), and on a practical level, the central organism created to put these laws into effect. I cannot but praise and encourage you in all this.

And it is within the framework of this program that you, Provincial Ministers, have wanted to assemble for two entire months in an ongoing formation course, that is, a more intense period of prayer, reflection and study. You have thus wanted to imitate in some way Christ who, "full of the Holy Spirit...was conducted by the Spirit into the desert for forty days" (Lk 4:1-2), and often retreated to pray. You have also wanted to imitate Saint Francis who spent long and frequent periods of retreat—especially during Lent—at Verna and other lonely places. You have felt the need for a spiritual renewal and for a cultural deepening, thus offering yourselves also as an example and incentive for your brothers.

181. Ongoing formation has been becoming ever more urgent and necessary in our days because of the continuous and multiple changes of our age, both in the civil field and in the more strictly religious one, changes which cause "such a rapid course of history that an individual person can scarcely keep abreast of it" (*Gaudium et Spes*, 5). Men are faced with new values or, at any rate, new ways of perceiving values. All of this demands a spirit that is closer to God and closer to men at the same time, a spirit attentive to the "voice of the Spirit" who speaks in the interior of consciences as in the "signs of the times." Thus the necessity for a spiritual life which is lived more deeply and a cultural preparation which makes you capable—in the light of the Gospel and of the Church's teaching—to respond to your vocation fully and to interpret the modern world correctly.

182. In a *letter* of mine *to all the priests of the Church*, after recalling two fundamental principles, that is, the necessity for conversion each day and the necessity for prayer "*sine intermissione*," I said: "We must link prayer with continuous work upon ourselves: *this is the 'formatio permanens'*[1] which must be at the same time interior, pastoral and intellectual.[2] This means that "since our pastoral activity, the proclamation of the Word and the whole of the priestly ministry depend upon the intensity of our *interior life*, that activity must also find sustenance in *assiduous study*. It is not enough for us to stop at what we once learned in the seminary, even in cases where those studies were done at university level.... This process of intellectual formation must last *all one's life*.... As teachers of the truth and of morals, we must tell men convincingly and effectively of the hope that gives us life. And this also forms part of *the process of daily conversion to love through the truth*."[3]

183. This doctrine of the Church is found in the new *Code of Canon Law* and is evident also in your *renewed Constitutions*, two documents which you certainly esteem and study with commitment.

Ongoing formation, in its two-fold dimension of continuous conversion and cultural updating, has as its goal a fuller and more consistent fidelity to one's vocation: "The effort of religious Institutes to update the objectives or methodologies would be futile if not inspired and accompanied by a deepening of and a new thrust to spirituality."[4]

I would like to emphasize *some objectives which must characterize your specific way* of carrying out ongoing formation.

184. First of all, the examination of that treasure which is the *fraternal life* to which you have been called. This value of brotherhood, so alive and true in the Saint of Assisi, has been considered by men of all times as a sublime ideal of human and community perfection. It is up to you in a special way to offer it with conviction, in deeds before words, in daily patient living, praying and working together.

In your history, the message of brotherhood has often been carried over into promoting peace agreements among public authorities—suffice it to recall the work for peace done by your brothers Lawrence of Brindisi and Mark of Aviano—as well as in the area of social tensions, through itinerant preaching and exercising the ministry of reconciliation, full of wisdom and good results in fervor and in simplicity, always on the basis of the Word of God. Saint Leopold, Blessed Jerome of Valacchia, Padre Pio, Padre Mariano of Turin, were proclaimers of love and therefore peacemakers (cf. Mt 5:9).

185. The charism of your Order, arising from the robust tree planted by Francis of Assisi, is characterized by the fervent practice of prayer, combined with that "pure joy" (Jas 1:2) which does not come from the world but from a profound contemplative communion with the crucified and risen Jesus.

If the path of these recent years has brought you to an apostolic activity which is perhaps too intense and diffusive, it is time to review your choices in this regard; give God more time and heart and mind; by your life teach the brothers that God has sacrosanct rights over man's existence and cannot be relegated to the last place in the house, to the last moment of the day. The search for intimacy with him must be the tireless commitment of your days.

186.   *The choice of the poor.* Today the world is discovering the presence of the poor with a new sense of responsibility. Often, however, this discovery remains on a theoretical level.

You have chosen the poor; and your Constitutions are there to remind you every day how to live the Lord's Beatitudes: "How blest are the poor in spirit: the reign of God is theirs" (Mt 5:3).

There will be different ways of identifying with the Lord's poor, but they will always be your chosen portion and the sharing of their suffering and hardship must always be a fundamental element of your life and work.

187.   By following these lines of conduct, you can be those witnesses of the Good News that the Church and men expect from you, according to the teachings and examples of Saint Francis.

You who are called and who are "the friars of the people" and have easier access to the heart of the lowly, can also more easily, especially through the itinerant apostolate, bring Jesus, man's Redeemer, into society, particularly to the large masses of the poor, the lowly, the weak.

The men of our times, upset by struggles and wars, by injustices and crises of every kind, need joy and hope, which can be drawn only from the divine Source. Refreshed by it every day, you too go throughout the world, like Francis, saying to everyone: "May the Lord give you peace!"[5] and proclaiming, as "guardians of hope," the salvation which comes from reconciliation with God.

188. The ministry of reconciliation is one of your great tasks, one of your glorious tasks! You must continue in the same glorious tradition. I think that you have the charism of confession, which you must always keep alive in your heart and in your ministry. This great, important charism! Especially in our times when, in human and Christian life, this charism becomes almost a bit abandoned on the one hand, but on the other hand is sought out! During the Synod so many bishops said that if there is a crisis regarding sacramental confession, it is also due to confessors who do not know how to hear confessions well. Now we must reverse this and rediscover love for confessions. And where are we to search for great lovers of confession if not in the Capuchin Order, especially after the canonization of Saint Leopold?

In this commitment, ever renewed, may Jesus the Divine Master guide you, and may the Virgin Mary, who kept and pondered the Word of the Lord in her heart (Lk 2:51), assist you.

May the Apostolic Blessing which I heartily impart to you descend upon you and upon the whole Capuchin Order.

---

[1] *Novo Incipiente*, Letter on the Occasion of Holy Thursday 1979, 10.

[2] Cf. Letter *Inter Ea* of the Sacred Congregation for the Clergy, November 4, 1969.

[3] *Novo Incipiente, ibid.*

[4] To the participants of the 106th General Chapter of the Third Order Regular of Saint Francis, May 19, 1983.

[5] Testament of Saint Francis.

20

TO THE GENERAL CHAPTER OF THE SALESIANS

April 3, 1984

189.   It gives me great joy to welcome to this special audience you who are the Major Superiors of the Salesian Society, on the occasion of your Twenty-Second General Chapter and on the day following a rather significant date: the fiftieth anniversary of the canonization of Saint John Bosco, your holy Founder, which occurred precisely on Easter Sunday, April 1, 1934, through the work of Pope Pius XI, who had personally known and esteemed him. . . .

190.   I would like to express the sincere congratulations of the whole Church for the work accomplished by the Salesians, beginning from that far-off day in 1858 when Don Bosco was here in the Apostolic Palace for the first time, in audience with Pius IX, to whom he presented a plan of rules for the Society he wanted to found! It was the beginning, small and hidden like the seed described by the Gospel, of the Society of Saint Francis de Sales, which was then officially realized with the definitive approval of the Constitutions in 1874, and which spread throughout the world, with admirable ranks of priests, missionaries, teachers, lay brothers, students and alumni, from Don Bosco's first successor, Blessed Don Rua, to the martyrs Monsignor Luigi Versiglia and Don Callisto Caravario, both of whom I had the joy of beatifying last year. A profound and sincere feeling of gratitude to the Lord must arise in your souls when you observe how, during this long period of years, in the midst of so many adverse and stormy events, Don Bosco has always remained present among you, in your houses, among the young people entrusted to you, in the

various initiatives and activities of your many institutions. The increase in vocations is also a reason for hope and consolation. Of course, for your Congregation too, there are difficult problems and complex issues; but it is very comforting for me to know that you are spurred on by the concern to be faithful to the spirit of Don Bosco, wherever you may be.

191.   Thus, together with my thanks for your visit and for the sentiments of fidelity and devotion which inspire it, I also add the strong exhortation to fervent and courageous perseverance. The revision of the Constitutions must be for you and for the entire Congregation a reason and an incentive for an ever more convinced and decisive apostolic commitment.

Let no one lose heart! Let no one let himself be dismayed in times of difficulty and possible defeats! Let no one allow himself to be conquered by the temptation to think his efforts are useless in the face of a secularized society which often forgets transcendent values! Remember what Don Bosco wrote to a disheartened parish priest: "Calm down then. Do not talk about freeing yourself from the parish. There is work to do! I will die working *'sicut bonus miles Christi'* (like a good soldier of Christ). Am I not good at much? *'Omnia possum in eo qui me confortat'* (I can do all things in him who strengthens me). Are there thorns? Angels will weave a crown in heaven for you with thorns changed into flowers. Are times difficult? They were always so, but God's help was never lacking. *'Christus heri et hodie'* (Christ yesterday and today)" (Turin, October 25, 1878).

192.   Never become discouraged! Look at Don Bosco, at his life, at his total dedication to souls! Read his writings; listen to his teaching, which is still valid; pray to him perseveringly and devoutly, so that his "spirit" may always be alive and present in you and in your educational, catechetical, parochial, athletic, recreational activities: "Everything for the Lord," he repeated. "Let us do what we can *'ad maiorem Dei gloriam'* (for the greater glory of God). We will rest in Paradise." Trained in the school of the

great saints and the great mystics, with daring and far-sightedness he kept the rudder of his life and his plan in hand and he was not afraid to affirm categorically: "I intend that all Salesians work for the Church until the last breath!" (Mem. B. XIV, 229). On December 7, 1887, expressing his last wishes to Monsignor Cagliero, he said: "May everyone work zealously and ardently: work, work! Always strive tirelessly to save souls!" (*ibid.*, XVIII, 477). In this regard, I like to offer the example of Cardinal August Hlond, Primate of Poland, spiritual son of Don Bosco, who had to suffer so much because of the tragic events of the last World War: "In the Salesian Congregation," he said, "I learned that work is neither a burden nor a cross, but a joy. . ." "Every brick is a cross, every stone a suffering. Tears cement them together. This is how the saints built. This is how Don Bosco built. I have placed all my confidence in Don Bosco and in Dominic Savio" (cf. *"A Shepherd of the Church during Difficult Times,"* Salesianum, no. 4, 1982).

193.   With regard to the work of the education and formation of youth, which is the Salesian Congregation's "charism," I ardently exhort you to desire to build on the firm rock of God's will, as Don Bosco did. It is important to emphasize and always keep in mind that Don Bosco's pedagogy had an extremely "eschatological" value and perspective: as Christ repeatedly said in the Gospel, it is essential to enter the Kingdom of heaven. But, paraphrasing Christ's words, neither mere sentimental invocation, nor ideological planning, nor social and utopian activism can give entrance to the Kingdom of heaven, but rather the fulfillment of God's will: the rains fall, the winds blow, the torrents come, they buffet that house, but it does not collapse because it is solidly set on rock (cf. Mt 7:21-27). Thus, it is necessary to erect the building of education also on the rock of God's will: this was the primary and constant intention of Don Bosco, who certainly cannot be accused of abstract mysticism or spiritual selfishness! And this must be the Salesians' never-ending commitment: God's will is certainly the knowledge of the person and message of Christ, the Revealer of the Father and the Redeemer

of mankind, as proclaimed by the apostles and taught by the Church; God's will is certainly the life of grace, and that is the Christocentric education which is pivoted on frequent confession and on the Eucharist. Today too, Don Bosco repeats to everyone: *"Memorare novissima tua et in aeternum non peccabis"* (Remember your last days and you will never sin) (Sir 7:36).

194. Young people today need and feel the necessity for spiritual, serious, enlightened, constructive guidance: this is the supreme responsibility of every priest and this is also his supreme joy! Families anxiously await your help, your collaboration, in "preventing" evil, in forming Christian consciences, in realizing the work of Redemption in "individuals." Don Bosco, that man so engaged in earthly values that he could so marvellously utilize his talents for dynamism and organization, could nevertheless be defined as "the man of eternity"! The will of God is certainly charity, which makes one totally fulfill his duty, obeying the authority of the Church and of one's superiors, and it expands one's heart to universal love. One day, Don Bosco gave this answer to young Prince Czartoryski, who turned to him as his spiritual director: "I pray. You pray too that God keep all of us steadfast on the road which can better assure Paradise for us" (*Epistolario*, vol. IV, 378). The supernatural view of existence is Don Bosco's radical teaching and it is the only way to build truly on the rock!

195. Reading the biography and writings of Saint John Bosco, one is impressed by the continuous reference to the presence of the Virgin Mary. It can be truly stated that he conceived everything and did everything in dependence on Mary and surrounded by her maternal and often even visible protection! In 1862 he confided to Don Cagliero: "Our Lady wants us to honor her under the title of Mary Help of Christians: times are so sad that we truly need the Virgin to help us preserve Christian faith." These are grave and serious words which we can repeat even today, strengthening our love and our trust in Mary Help of Christians

ever more. Put your trust in Mary! Every day entrust all your activities and your anxieties to her maternal care!

With the wish that your Chapter decisions bear abundant and effective fruits, I impart my Blessing to you, which I willingly extend to the entire Salesian Congregation.

21

TO THE GENERAL CHAPTER OF THE
CHRISTIAN BROTHERS

April 12, 1984

196.   It gives me great pleasure to welcome you as members of the Twenty-Sixth General Chapter of the Congregation of the Christian Brothers. I greet you with the words of the Apostle Paul: "I thank my God through Jesus Christ for all of you, because *your faith is proclaimed in all the world*" (Rom 1:8).

You represent almost three thousand Christian Brothers actively involved in the education of youth in over three hundred and fifty communities on the five continents. Moreover, you are the bearers of a truly glorious tradition of commitment to the education of the young which had its humble origin in the first school that your Founder, Edmund Ignatius Rice, set up in a stable at Waterford in the early years of the nineteenth century. That was indeed an act of *evangelical compassion,* moved as he was by the pitiable state of young boys who had no prospect of education or guidance in the sad conditions of poverty and extreme religious discrimination in which they lived.

Who can measure the extent of the good achieved by your Congregation since then? How many boys have grown to Christian maturity in their personal and professional lives, as a result of the often unspoken heroism of the work carried out by the Brothers with that deep personal faith, with the spirit of self-dedication, and the inner joy that characterizes the followers of Edmund Ignatius Rice?

197.   Your General Chapter has the important task of revising the Constitutions and other regulations to be submitted for the approval of the Sacred Congregation

for Religious and for Secular Institutes. You are also engaged in a process of renewal and adaptation.

In this respect I would draw your attention to what I said in my recent Apostolic Exhortation, *Redemptionis Donum:* "The Church thinks of you, above all, as persons who are 'consecrated': *consecrated to God in Jesus Christ* as his exclusive possession" (no. 7).

Without doubt, the effectiveness of your apostolate and the vitality of your Congregation, indeed the sense of personal identity and therefore the spiritual maturity of each member of your Congregation, depend upon the authentic way in which this *consecration* is accepted and lived.

198.   As members of a Religious Institute you have a specific witness to give. You proclaim the saving power of Christ by your particular style of life, which is based on the observance of the evangelical counsels and animated by a solid piety that is at once personal and common to all the members of the Congregation.

199.   Allow me to mention briefly one aspect of Christian piety which contributes greatly to the attainment of holiness and the consistency of your witness. I refer to the intense devotion to the Blessed Sacrament that marked the spiritual journey of Edmund Rice and from which so much strength and enlightenment has come for innumerable members of his Congregation. You must be men of frequent contact with the risen Christ in the Sacrament of his presence, in order to nourish the faith that sustains and gives meaning to your vocation.

The Second Vatican Council took pains to point out that the fact must be honestly faced: that even the most desirable changes made in view of contemporary needs will fail to achieve their purpose unless *a renewal of spirit*—an interior renewal of the heart—gives life to them (cf. *Perfectae Caritatis,* 2).

200.   You have wished to visit the Pope. And I take this opportunity to thank you for your specific ecclesial service in fostering the integral development of youth. I appreciate too the direct assistance given by the Congregation of the Christian Brothers to the Holy See.

May I also ask you for something? You are well aware of the needs of the Church all over the world in relation to vocations to the priesthood and to the religious life. My request is that you do not fail to challenge the young to follow Christ in this way. Help them to discover the divine call. Support them by your prayer, your advice, and the example of your lives.

It is my ardent hope that you will be encouraged by this meeting to continue along the path of fidelity to the original inspiration of your Founder. I pray that your Congregation will grow and flourish with new vocations; that the lives of all its members will be fruitful and fulfilled in the task entrusted to each one.

May the Blessed Virgin Mary, Queen of Apostles, protect you and inspire you by her example of perfect consecration!

Praised be Jesus Christ!

22

TO THE OBLATES OF SAINT FRANCES
OF ROME, IN ROME

April 29, 1984

201.   "Peace be with you" (Jn 20:19), beloved Oblates of
        Saint Frances of Rome! With this greeting of the
risen Christ, which we heard in the liturgy of this Sunday
in Albis, I wish to express to you my deep joy and my satisfaction in being among you in this ancient monastery, in
this island of the spirit, which for centuries has been for
Rome a continual reminder of the transcendent values of
faith, hope and charity.

        My visit allows me also to show you my apprecia-
tion for you personally and for the choice that you have
made for your lives, consecrating yourselves totally to
Christ and his Church, according to the charism of your
renowned Foundress. You are celebrating the sixth
centenary of her birth of the noble Bussa de' Leoni family
in Rome.

        My coming coincides also with the ceremony of the
sacred vows which you have renewed today as a sign of your
continued fidelity to God and the Church. For this very significant religious act also, I express my satisfaction and encouragement that you will be able to continue to offer, with
the same enthusiasm as the first days of your entry into
this place of perfection, your witness of a religious and evangelical life in this diocese of Rome, so loved by your holy
Foundress that she deserved to be called "Roman," this diocese so thirsty for God and desirous of giving an ever clearer
and more consistent meaning to its choices in view of eternal life.

202.   Your Foundress' centenary year has already afforded
        me the opportunity to open my heart in a letter
addressed to you last January and to evoke once more her

shining and exemplary figure as a wife, a mother, and a religious, and particularly her prodigious activity on behalf of the poor, the sick, the oppressed in the Rome of the early Renaissance, deeply divided among opposing factions and sorely tried by profound moral and social evils. The charitable work that the Saint carried out for the relief of the needy of Rome was so admirable that it won for her the honorable title of *Advocata Urbis*.

On this occasion I wish to continue that meditation and exhort you, after the example of your Foundress, never to desist in your striving toward the *perfection* to which the Lord calls you in the words recorded in the Gospel: "Be perfect, as your heavenly Father is perfect" (Mt 5:48). Christian perfection requires continual vigilance, an incessant opening to God and to neighbor. It is therefore not authentic if it is not enlivened by charity; if the religious mentality slowly yields to the attractions of earthly things, neglecting spiritual and eternal things; if the consecrated soul forgets the great problems of the Church and the world; in a word, if the mystery of the dead and risen Christ is not lived to the full.

203.　May this anniversary be an incentive to renew sentiments, ideas and resolutions according to the spirit of the Benedictine Order of Mount Olivet. Be tenaciously faithful to the main lines of your monastic tradition and devoutly observe the Rule of Saint Benedict, which was the inspiration for your venerated Foundress in giving to your community its rules of life. Appreciate their wise discretion and human flexibility, responding to the needs of monastic life and at the same time to the needs of the time. Do not cease to probe their intimate inspiration, destined to be an evangelical ferment for anyone who undertakes their observance. Do not disappoint the expectations and hopes that the Foundress placed in her Oblates.

May your light be the way mapped out by your Mother in the specific commitment to prayer, sacrifice, and works for the Church and for the city of Rome, adapting yourselves to the needs of the times. Just as the Oblates cared for the poorest in the early centuries, carried out educational activity for the youth in the seventeenth and eighteenth centuries, and engaged in missionary cooperation in the nineteenth century, so you today, in a particular way, take care of the education of youth and of catechesis in the parish environment.

204.   Beloved Oblates, it is not possible for me to stay longer with you. But I am sure I can count on your interior intuition which will be able to gather and develop the seeds of reflection that I have just mentioned. At every moment of your day, made up of work, silence, humility and obedience, may the Lord find you ready, like the wise virgins, to meet him with your torches lit (cf. Mt 25:10).

May the holy Virgin Mary, whose name you bear, guide you, and may the Apostolic Blessing, which I heartily impart to you and your loved ones, strengthen your resolutions.

23

TO THE CLERGY, AND MEN AND WOMEN RELIGIOUS IN SEOUL

May 5, 1984

205.   "Blessed are those who are persecuted for righteousness' sake, for theirs is the Kingdom of heaven" (Mt 5:10). The truth of these words of our Savior, *the truth of the Beatitudes, is manifested in the heroic witness of the Korean Martyrs.* For these holy men, women and children who suffered cruel persecution and death are blessed indeed. They are a sign of the power of God transforming the timid and weak into brave witnesses to Christ. Because they submitted to death for the sake of the Gospel, they have received a great reward in heaven and are honored by the Church throughout the world. In the presence of the Redeemer, they rejoice and are glad, for they were "counted worthy to suffer for the sake of the name of Jesus" (cf. Acts 5:41).

206.   The truth of the Beatitudes is also manifested *in the priesthood and religious life,* for these are *a particular incarnation of the Beatitudes.* As priests and religious you bear witness to what it means to be blessed by God. In your celibacy or consecrated chastity, embraced out of love for Christ, you show your trust in his words: "Blessed are the pure in heart, for they shall see God" (Mt 5:8). By your evangelical poverty lived in generous service to others, you proclaim again the first Beatitude: "Blessed are the poor in spirit, for theirs is the Kingdom of heaven" (Mt 5:3). And in so many different ways, individually and in union with others, you seek to incarnate the Beatitudes, to live a life which gives convincing proof that the Beatitudes are indeed true, that they are the sure path to holiness.

207.   I wish for a moment to direct my words to *my brother priests*. One of the greatest joys of coming to Korea is that I am able, here in your land, to canonize your Martyrs. Among them are priests, including your first Korean priest, Father Andrew Kim Taegon. The historic event of the canonization draws attention to the illustrious Christian heritage that is yours. At the same time, it stirs up in your own hearts a greater zeal for holiness, a desire to imitate the martyrs in your own specific way.

Remember, dear brothers, that *priestly holiness means being like Christ: it means doing the Father's will;* it means faithfully exercising your pastoral ministry. You are called to "live by faith in the Son of God" (Gal 2:20) and to love the Word of God. Each day you nourish your mind and heart at the table of the Word so richly provided by the Church in the celebration of the Eucharist and the Liturgy of the Hours. This Word of God moves you to praise God's name with joyful hearts and to obey his commands and counsels. It spurs you on to an ever more generous service of your people, in proclaiming the Gospel of salvation and leading the faithful in prayer.

208.   As you seek to give a shepherd's care to the portion of God's flock entrusted to you, you must have a special love for the poor and the outcasts, for those who are forgotten, for those who are sick or burdened by their own sins. You are called to give a generous part of your time to celebrating the Sacrament of Penance, and to instructing your people in its value and importance for their Christian lives. Never doubt the effectiveness of the *ministry of confession*. Through you the Lord Jesus himself reconciles hearts to himself and pours out his mercy and love. And you too are called to experience Christ's mercy and love and to bear witness to your faith by your personal use of this great sacrament.

209.   It is above all *to the Eucharist that all your pastoral activities are directed* and from which God's richest graces flow. The Second Vatican Council gives us the magnificent assurance that "in the mystery of the Eucharistic

Sacrifice, in which priests fulfill their principal function, the work of our Redemption is continually carried out" (*Presbyterorum Ordinis,* 13).

210. And now, I wish to speak to the *men and women religious* of Korea, to you for whom God has a special love, and the Church a special esteem. Dear brothers and sisters, as religious you share in a particular way in the mission of Christ. By your personal and liturgical prayer and by the specific charisms of your Institutes, you fulfill a unique and important role in the Church. Above all, it is given to you *to bear witness to Jesus Christ* who was always obedient to the Father and who became poor that we might become rich.

211. Some of you have been called to the *contemplative* form of religious life, in which, through prayer and penance as your specific role, you seek an ever more intimate communion with God in charity. In this way you exemplify the Church as the spotless Bride of Christ, and your very lives lived in union with Jesus take on the power of a continuous act of intercession for God's people. Others of you are called to dedicate yourselves with no less zeal to *the various works of the apostolate.* In hospitals and in schools, in parishes and in specialized fields of service, you bear witness to Christ and, together with the laity and the clergy, collaborate in the one mission of the Church. Whatever type of religious life the Lord Jesus has called you to, by reason of your religious consecration you share in his Passion, death and Resurrection in a special way.

212. Jesus said: "Unless a grain of wheat falls into the earth and dies, it remains alone; but if it dies, it bears much fruit" (Jn 12:24). Religious life, like martyrdom, is a special invitation from God to become this grain of wheat, to trust that *dying in Christ* brings forth abundant fruit and leads to eternal life. Together with all the baptized, but in a fuller way by reason of your religious consecration, you share in our Savior's Cross. As you strive to accept joyfully the daily trials of life and the difficulties

inherent in human work and social relationships, be confident that the Cross when embraced out of love for Christ is always a tree of new life. The great charism of religious life is generous love—generous love of Christ and the members of his Body. It is expressed in service and consummated in sacrifice. You are willing to give in proportion to your love, and when love is perfect the sacrifice is complete.

213.   I invite all of you to join me today in expressing *gratitude* to God and in praising him *for the many vocations to the priesthood and religious life* which have characterized the Church in Korea in recent years. Here is a sign of the *vitality of your faith*; it is likewise a sign of *the power of Christ's Paschal Mystery* and the efficacy of his Precious Blood. Indeed, the Church in your land cannot even be imagined without your vital presence in parishes, schools, hospitals and other specialized fields of apostolic endeavor. And your service offers great hope for the future, not only for the Church in your land but for other countries as well which will receive missionaries from Korea. The universal Church counts on your missionary contribution.

214.   I encourage you to pray for more vocations, and to try continually to foster them among the people whom you serve. Ask the Korean Martyrs to intercede for this special intention, which is so important for the future of the Church. And may your lives which are an incarnation of the Beatitudes be eloquent signs of the presence of Jesus Christ in the world.

215.   In a word, dear priests and religious, millions of your brethren in Korea, including countless non-Christians, are speaking to you in those words that were addressed to the apostle Philip in Jerusalem: "We wish to see Jesus" (Jn 12:21). Yes, my brothers and sisters, you must *show Jesus* to your people; you must *share Jesus* with your people: the praying Jesus, the Jesus of the Beatitudes, the

Jesus who, in you, wishes to be obedient and poor, meek, humble and merciful, pure, peaceful, patient and just. This is the Jesus whom you represent: the eternal Son of the Father who became incarnate in the womb of the Virgin Mary and who wishes to be visible in you. The Jesus of the Paschal Mystery, who, in the power of his Spirit and through the cooperation of his Church, longs to lead all humanity to his Father.

This is the *solemn challenge of your lives: show Jesus* to the world; *share Jesus* with the world.

24

TO THE CLERGY, RELIGIOUS,
AND LAY LEADERS, IN PORT MORESBY

May 8, 1984

216.   Beloved faithful people of Port Moresby and Papua New Guinea:

Jesus Christ, the Son of God, "died for all, that those who live might live no longer for themselves but for him who for their sake died and was raised" (2 Cor 5:15).

My brothers and sisters in Christ, the Redemption of the world was accomplished by the Passion, death and Resurrection of our Lord Jesus Christ. Before the Redemption, mankind was enslaved by sin, inclined to dominate rather than serve, living for self and not for others. But by the mystery of his Cross and Resurrection, we have been given *the freedom and grace to live no longer for ourselves but for him.* What a wonderful gift from Christ, our Savior!

It was precisely for this reason that *Christ died* for all of us, to liberate us from the bond of selfishness from which by ourselves we could never escape, *to make us free,* and to enable us to live for him. This is the gift which Christ won for all of us: clergy, religious, laity. It is the gift which the missionaries brought to Papua New Guinea, which they carried in their own hearts and which they put into practice in this land. I think of the example of *Blessed Giovanni Mazzucconi,* who gave his life for love of Christ. His martyrdom is an eloquent proclamation of the teaching of Jesus which we have heard in today's Gospel: "Whoever of you does not renounce all that he has cannot be my disciple" (Lk 14:33).

217.   Through the living waters of Baptism, all of us have received the grace of living for Christ. Thus we have been made sharers in the work which he himself came to accomplish, namely, to reconcile the world to God. As we

have heard in today's first reading: *"God... through Christ reconciled us to himself and gave us the ministry of reconciliation"* (2 Cor 5:18).

All members of the Church share in the "ministry of reconciliation," but each according to the gifts that he or she has received.

218. The *laity,* by their daily witness to Christ at home, at work and in all the ordinary circumstances of the world, wrestle against the hostility and divisions which still exist in a society marked by sin, and *seek to build a Kingdom* of truth and justice, the Kingdom of the living God—a Kingdom of love and peace.

Married couples make an important contribution to the unity and stability of society by remaining faithful to their promises of lifelong fidelity and by bearing witness to the generous love of Christ for his Spouse, the Church. And *the Christian family,* united in faith and prayer, is like *a school where the lessons of forgiveness,* patience and love for one another are learned. In the family, children are prepared to take their part in the life and mission of the Church.

Lay leaders and catechists also serve as "ambassadors for Christ," seeking to promote harmony and peace. Here in Papua New Guinea, your apostolic efforts have been vitally needed to hand on the message of the Gospel to your brothers and sisters. And therefore I wish to commend you for your generosity and fidelity and for the way you work in close collaboration with the clergy and religious.

219. *Men and women religious,* by their religious consecration, play a special role in the Church's ministry of reconciliation. In their desire to love Christ with an undivided heart (cf. 1 Cor 7:35), they *bear public witness to the Gospel of Redemption and reconciliation.* That is why it is so important for each community of religious to be united among themselves, to be "of one heart and soul" (Acts 4:32). Dear religious: this lived unity among

yourselves, which underlies your public witness to the Gospel, is strengthened by your common life and prayer, and by your sacred vows, especially the vow of obedience.

220.   Always remember that sin and division first entered the world "by one man's disobedience," but reconciliation was restored "by one man's obedience" (Rom 5:19), *the obedience of Jesus.* Therefore when you imitate Christ through the obedience you give to him and to the Church through your religious superiors, you are contributing to the Church's ministry of reconciliation. As I stated in my recent Apostolic Exhortation to Men and Women Religious: "It can therefore be said that those who decide to live according to the counsel of obedience are placed in a unique way between *the mystery of sin* and the mystery *of justification and salvific grace. . .* Precisely by means of the vow of obedience they decide *to be transformed* into the likeness of Christ, who 'redeemed humanity and made it holy by his obedience.' In the counsel of obedience they desire to find their own role in the Redemption of Christ and their own way of sanctification" (*Redemptionis Donum*, 13).

221.   And now, I would like to say a word to *my brother priests.* The words of Saint Paul in the first reading this afternoon have a special meaning for us who share in the ordained ministry. The Apostle says, "In Christ God was reconciling the world to himself. . . and *entrusting to us the message of reconciliation*" (2 Cor 5:19). As men chosen to proclaim the Word of God, as priests strengthened for this noble task by the Sacrament of Holy Orders, we must place our whole lives at the service of the Word, letting Christ make "his appeal through us. . . be reconciled to God" (2 Cor 5:20).

222.   Working in *hierarchical communion* with the local bishop, priests strive to build up the unity of the local Christian community, and to cultivate a fraternal spirit which embraces not only the local Church but the universal Church as well. Because the service of unity is so vital in today's world, it is even more urgent that

priests themselves should never create division through their activities, but rather should strive to unite the community by offering to the faithful the Word of God.

223.   Above all, dear brothers, you must foster reconciliation in the Church and in the world through your attentive ministry of the *Sacrament of Penance* and the *celebration of the Eucharist.* Never doubt the great value of the time you spend hearing confessions. It is a time when, in a unique way, you represent the merciful Redeemer who rejoices at the conversion of sinners. And also remember the words of the Second Vatican Council: "No Christian community can be built up unless it has its basis and center in the celebration of the most Holy Eucharist" (*Presbyterorum Ordinis,* 6).

224.   In the Gospel passage this evening we heard Jesus speak of someone "desiring to build a tower" (Lk 14:28). He warned of the importance of carefully calculating the cost before deciding to build; otherwise people would begin to mock the builder saying, "This man began to build, and was not able to finish" (Lk 14:30).

Dear brothers and sisters in Christ, we too desire to build something in union with Jesus our Redeemer. We desire *to build the Kingdom* of the living God. In our desire, let us not forget to *calculate the cost,* the cost of building the Kingdom, the cost of discipleship. For Jesus warned us: "Whoever does not bear his own cross and come after me, cannot be my disciple" (Lk 14:27).

225.   In order to live for Christ and no longer for ourselves, to collaborate in the ministry of reconciliation, to build the Kingdom of God, *we must bear the cross* and follow Jesus. Let us not be afraid to be signs of contradiction. Let us embrace the cross, confident that it is a "tree of eternal life," trusting in the firm promise of the resurrection.

Together with the Virgin Mary and all the saints, let us build God's Kingdom here on earth, so as to be able to live for ever with the Father and the Son and the Holy Spirit. Amen.

25

TO THE CLERGY, RELIGIOUS AND LAITY, IN BANGKOK

May 11, 1984

226.   Grace, mercy and peace be with you from God the Father and from Jesus Christ, the Father's Son, in truth and love (cf. 2 Jn 1:3).

I have been greatly looking forward to this meeting with you, priests, religious and lay men and women. I have been eager to greet you who have such an important role in *the evangelization and ecclesial life of Thailand*. So very often, from the See of Peter, the Prince of Apostles, whose tomb is preserved under the main altar of the Vatican Basilica, my thoughts have reached out to you: "I do not cease to give thanks for you, remembering you in my prayers" (Eph 1:16).

In the context of the pastoral motives of my brief visit to your country, *I give special importance to this meeting*. You, in fact, have been entrusted, according to your different roles, with the task of *shepherding Christ's flock* in union with the Bishops, and of offering a clear and unambiguous *testimony of Christian life* that will nourish the People of God and speak to the hearts and consciences of all men and women of good will.

227.   "I do not cease to give thanks for you": in the first place, for the *numerous vocations* to the priesthood which the Father has raised up in the Church in Thailand. I also give thanks for the vitality of the many religious Congregations that bear witness to the fruitful charisms that the Spirit of Christ has poured out on the Church in this land. I thank God for the fortitude and perseverance of the laity in their Christian lives. And I thank all of you, and your brothers and sisters who have not been able to be present here today, for the generous and faithful response

which you have given—either as priests, religious or laity—to the call received from God. I pray that I may fulfill Peter's task to confirm you in the faith: that you may live by faith in the Son of God who loved you and gave himself for you (cf. Gal 2:20): that you may be faithful to your calling and never lose sight of the great privilege that is yours: to collaborate in communicating Christ to the world and to build his Kingdom of holiness, justice and love.

228.   As you are well aware, the privilege of a Christian vocation demands a *full response*. It requires every day a confirmation of your original "yes" to the invitation of Christ. It requires a renewal of your baptismal commitment, a renewal of your religious consecration and the promises of your priesthood. May your joy be to follow to the end the road on which you have embarked in following Jesus Christ, the Son of God and Savior of the world.

229.   I am aware of the many and varied ways in which you carry out your service to God's people. Among your activities, however, there is a difference that corresponds to your specific vocation.

First I wish to say a word to you, the priests. In a special way, you must heed the teaching of the Acts of the Apostles. The first disciples considered their principal task to be their devotion "to prayer and to the ministry of the Word" (Acts 6:4). You are privileged to have daily contact with Christ through *personal and liturgical prayer*. It is especially in the faith-filled celebration of the sacraments—chief among them the Eucharistic Sacrifice, which is "the source and summit of the whole Christian life" (*Lumen Gentium*, 11)—that you will draw joy and strength. In prayerful meditation on the revealed *Word of God*, you will find "constant and familiar companionship with the Father" (*Optatam Totius*, 8), through his Son, Jesus Christ. In this way you will become better instruments of the power of the Holy Spirit to build up God's people into a holy dwelling place for God: "For we are God's fellow workers" (1 Cor 3:9).

230.   Your service to the Word includes the task of ade-
        quately *catechizing* your Christian communities so
that they may live their faith in a mature and responsible
way. This requires that you make time available for study
and that you strive constantly to follow the injunction of
the First Letter of Peter: "Be always prepared to make a
defense to any one who calls you to account for the hope
that is in you, with gentleness and reverence" (1 Pt 3:15-16).
Nor can you overlook your task to present appropriately
the *first proclamation of the Christian message* to those who
have not yet been comforted by the Gospel of Christ.

231.   The communication of the Good News must be ac-
        companied by *the example of a life* that finds its in-
spiration in Jesus himself. Allow me, dear priests, to say
to you what Saint Paul wrote to the Philippians: "Only let
your manner of life be worthy of the Gospel of Christ, so
that whether I come and see you or am absent, I may hear
of you that you stand firm in one spirit, with one mind striving side by side for the faith of the Gospel" (Phil 1:27). I
assure you that this is my daily prayer for you!

232.   The duty of being living examples of the Christian
        life belongs, too, in a specific way, to the religious
of the Church. Dear religious: in you who have been consecrated to the Lord, the believers and unbelievers of this
world expect to see that special love that Christ taught as
his "new" commandment: "By this all men will know that
you are my disciples, if you have love for one another" (Jn
13:35). *The charity of Christ*, the pillar and support of your
life in community and the power of your apostolic activities, will be the most effective proclamation of the truth
of the Gospel, giving inner strength and vitality to the
Church in Thailand. I wish to assure you of my affection,
and to tell you how confidently I place my hopes in you!

233.   In the communion that is the Church, the laity have
        their own specific and indispensable part to play.
And to you, dear lay people, I say: by reason of your baptismal incorporation into Christ you share actively, and in a

manner all your own, in the responsibility of *transforming the world* according to the truth and values of the Gospel. It is your task to live in such a way that your Christian faith will overflow into the social, cultural, professional and everyday human activities in which you are engaged. The Church in Thailand needs your active collaboration very much! The challenge of providing abundant and efficient educational, social and fraternal services weighs heavily on your shoulders. By meeting this challenge you build up the Kingdom of God in a visible way and at the same time make a very valuable contribution to the *development and well-being of your country.* Be assured of the Pope's blessing and support! Take my greetings to your families and communities, especially to the young and the old, and to those who suffer any kind of need!

234.   Dear priests, religious and lay men and women: your various vocations are different. Each, in its own way, manifests the deep richness of Christ's redemptive mission at work in the Church. Every vocation and every ecclesial task has its source of life and energy in *the celebration of the Eucharist.* Christ calls you to meet each other and to draw strength for your apostolates at the table of the Word and of his Body and Blood.

I am pleased to know that special efforts are being made to make *the treasures of the liturgy* more accessible to the faithful. This will greatly nourish the spiritual life of the Church in Thailand. I hope that more and more lay persons will be able to share in the praying of the Liturgy of the Hours, which is the hymn of praise addressed to God by Christ and by the *whole Church.* This prayer of the Church belongs to all the People of God.

235.   Your encounter with Christ in the liturgy and in personal prayer becomes the point of departure for the fulfillment of *your missionary vocation.* For the entire Church is called upon to be missionary. All the Church's members share this task, and not only the brothers and sisters that local Churches in other parts of the world have

sent to you, as a living sign of ecclesial communion and catholicity.

And to you, *missionaries* from other countries, I express an especially cordial greeting! Accept the thanks of the Church and of the Pope for the gift that you have made of yourselves to the Church in Thailand! The Lord Jesus himself accepts your offering and presents it to his Father in union with his own.

236.   The whole Church in Thailand must be missionary: not out of a spirit of competition, or out of a desire to impose points of view different from the traditional values of the remarkable cultural tradition of this people; but only out of the need *to share* both the divine life that the Holy Spirit nourishes in you and in the joy that is yours in Christ.

May our Father in heaven become known, through you, *in the very values* that characterize your Thai culture! May the Holy Spirit form Jesus Christ in you, and through your lives and teaching communicate him to the world. May Mary, the Mother of our Divine Savior, be forever the cause of your joy!

26

LETTER TO THE MINISTER GENERAL
OF THE ORDER OF CARTHUSIANS

May 14, 1984

237.   "To attend to silence and to the solitude of the cell,"
such is the work and the aim by which one recognizes the Order of Carthusians, at the head of which you
find yourself (cf. Revised Statutes of the Carthusian Order,
4, 1). Its members, in response to an altogether special call
from God and in order to live for him alone, have passed
"from the tempest of this world to the security and repose
of a well-sheltered harbor" (Saint Bruno, *Lettre à Raoul,*
in "Lettres des premiers Chartreux," Sources chretiennes,
Paris, 1962, p. 74).

For nine hundred years now, your Order has endea-
vored to lead, with an admirable perseverance and energy,
this "life hidden with Christ" (cf. Col 3:3). It is appropriate to draw attention to this during these days when we
celebrate the anniversary of your foundation. This took
place, in fact, around the 24th of June, 1084, the day consecrated to Saint John the Baptist, "the greatest of the
prophets and the friend of the desert" (cf. Hymn at Lauds
on the Solemnity of the Birth of Saint John the Baptist),
he whom the Carthusians honor as heavenly patron after
the Virgin Mary. Saint Bruno, that eminent man, and some
companions, began then this form of life separated from
the world in a place called the Chartreuse, situated in the
diocese of Grenoble. Uniting our joy with yours at the
remembrance of this happy event, from the depths of our
heart we congratulate you on such a long-standing fidelity and we wish to profit of this occasion to manifest to the
entire Carthusian family our very particular esteem and
our paternal affection.

238.   It is well known that, in the first centuries of the
        Church, hermits lived in desert places, devoted to
prayer and to work. "Stripped of everything, they gave their
name to a wholly heavenly way of life" (Saint Athanasius,
Life of Saint Anthony, PG 26,866); it is they who were at
the origin of the religious life. Their examples incited admiration and drew many men along the path of virtue.
Saint Jerome, to cite one testimony among so many others,
proclaimed in glowing terms the hidden secret of the
monks: "O desert, dotted with the flowers of Christ! O solitude, where the stones are born with which, in the
Apocalypse, the city of the great King is built! O secluded
spots, where one enjoys God more intimately! (*Letter* 14, PL
22, 353-354).

239.   Many a time the Roman Pontiffs have approved this
        life separated from men and were not sparing in
their praises of it. For what concerns you, in the contemporary epoch, it was the Apostolic Constitution "Umbrati-
lem" of Pius XI, then a letter sent to you yourself by Paul
VI on the occasion of your General Chapter of Renewal
(*AAS,* 16, [1924], p. 385 ff.; 63, [1971], p. 447 ff.). For its part,
Vatican Council II expressed its esteem for the solitary life,
whose adherents more closely follow Christ contemplating
on the mountain, and it affirmed that this life is a hidden
source of fruitfulness for the Church (cf. *Lumen Gentium,*
46; *Perfectae Caritatis,* 7). Finally, the new Code of Canon
Law has just strongly confirmed this teaching: "Institutes
wholly ordered to contemplation always retain a distinguished position in the Mystical Body of Christ" (Can. 674).

240.   All of that concerns you, dear Carthusian monks and
        nuns, who, far from the uproar of the world, "have
chosen the better part" (cf. Lk 10:42). Faced with the ac-
celeration of the rhythm of life which sweeps along our contemporaries, you must unceasingly return to the primitive
spirit of your Order, and remain unshakable in your holy
vocation. Our age, in fact, seems to need your example and
your service: minds are torn between diverse opinions; very
often they are perturbed, they even run the risk of great

spiritual dangers under the pressure of multiple writings which appear without discernment, and above all from the means of social communications, which are endowed with such a great power of influencing hearts while sometimes being in opposition to Christian truth and morality. Men experience then the need to set out on a quest for the absolute and to see it vouched for by a lived witness. Your duty is precisely to help them perceive it.

241.   For their part, the sons and daughters of the Church who consecrate themselves to the apostolate in the midst of the world, grappling with the perpetual instability and evolution of things, must lean on the stability of God and his love. They contemplate this stability manifest in you, who have it most especially as your portion here below.

The Church herself, as the Mystical Body of Christ, owes it to herself to offer continually a sacrifice of praise to the Divine Majesty, and this is one of her principal responsibilities; in virtue of this, she counts on your devoted zeal, you who, each day, "mount guard in the presence of God" (cf. Saint Bruno, *ibid.*, p. 68).

242.   Let us acknowledge, however, that in our age, when one gives oneself over, perhaps too easily, to action, your eremitical life is sometimes misunderstood or underestimated, above all in view of the shortage of laborers for the Lord's vineyard. Contrary to such opinions, it is necessary to affirm that the Carthusians must integrally preserve, even today, the authentic traits of their Order. This is in accord with the rule formulated by the new Code of Canon Law: while recalling the urgent needs of the active apostolate, it defends the specific character of the vocation of those who belong to purely contemplative Institutes; and this by reason of the service that these religious render to the People of God, "moving it by their example and contributing to its extension through their hidden apostolic fruitfulness" (Can. 674). If, for this reason,

the members of your family "cannot be summoned to aid in various pastoral ministries"(*ibid.*), neither do you have to exercise, at least in a habitual manner, that other form of apostolate whereby persons from the exterior are welcomed who desire to make several days' retreat in your monasteries, because that would correspond poorly to the purpose of the eremitical life.

243.   One cannot doubt that the numerous and rapid changes taking place in contemporary society, the new psychological consequences which influence minds, especially those of youth, and the nervous tension that afflicts so many people today, can bring about difficulties in Carthusian communities, principally among those who present themselves as candidates to your Order. You must act with prudence and firmness—at the same time striving to take into account the problems of the young—so as to preserve your true charism in its integrality, without deviating from your recognized statutes. Only a will on fire with the love of God and disposed to serve him valiantly will be able to surmount these obstacles.

244.   Behold the Church so near to you, dear sons and daughters of Saint Bruno; she counts on the numerous spiritual fruits resulting from your prayers and the austerities that you endure for the love of God. We have already had the occasion to say, in order to clarify the sense of a life consecrated to God: "It is not what you do that matters most, but what you are" (cf. Allocution to Priests and Men and Women Religious, *AAS,* 71, [1979], p. 1127)[1]: this seems to apply most particularly to you, who keep yourselves apart from what is called the active life.

Therefore, while you go over in your hearts the origins of your family, you cannot but feel moved to a renewal of interior ardor and spiritual joy in giving yourself without reserve to your sublime vocation.

As a sign of the love which has inspired these lines and as a pledge of abundant graces from heaven, we are happy in the Lord to accord our Apostolic Blessing to you, dear son, as well as to all the monks and nuns of the Carthusian Order.

At the Vatican, May 14, 1984, the sixth year of our pontificate.

---

[1] Cf. Book I—no. 191.

27

TO WOMEN RELIGIOUS IN VITERBO (ITALY)

May 27, 1984

245.   First of all, I thank your bishop for the warm and affectionate words with which he has introduced this meeting of ours, and I want to express my deep joy to be here among you, beloved sisters, to recall with gratitude to God the important anniversaries of two great figures of women who have, with their example of sanctity, distinguished and still distinguish the history of Viterbo: the seven-hundred-fiftieth anniversary of the birth of Saint Rose and the four-hundredth of the birth of Saint Hyacintha Marescotti.

Dear religious of the contemplative and active lives here present, what more beautiful occasion than the commemoration of these two saints to meditate briefly together, in the light of their ever-relevant witness, on the meaning and the value of the religious vocation?

246.   To think and to rethink with lucidity about this great theme of the Christian life is never useless, because continually, and I should say almost every day, it is necessary to defend this very lofty value against a persistent series of perils, sometimes rather subtle, by means of which the spirit of evil would like to destroy it.

Saint Rose and Saint Hyacintha, as for that matter every soul who wants to truly follow Christ, above all when it comes to the consecrated life, teach us with their lives what I could define as the "joyful seriousness" of the commitment which is assumed before God when one answers his call: joy, because of the awareness of the special love of which one is unworthily the object; seriousness, knowing that this call concretely involves the *total direction of our existence.* The Christian and baptismal vocation, and even more the religious one, which is a development of it, touch the *innermost part of our being before God.* By our attitude—positive or negative—toward it, *we put our eternal destiny into play.*

247. But what does this presume? Obviously the capacity to place our existence in relation with the absolute, with the eternal, that is—in the last analysis—with God. In other words, it presumes the capacity to discover completely that image of God which is in us and which rather *we are.* It is only by accepting with a special attitude of listening this "spark" of the eternal which is in our spirit—the divine call—that, overcoming the transient and the incidental, we can make that *final decision* regarding the meaning of our existence, a decision which is both an act of confidence in divine help, and a sign of *true human maturity.* In this free binding of oneself to God *forever*—it is understood after a period of careful verification—we reach the true freedom and completeness of our personality, in a human sense even before the Christian. In fact, as I said in my Encyclical *Redemptor Hominis* (no. 21): "Mature humanity means full use of the gift of freedom... This gift finds its full realization in the unreserved giving of the whole of one's human person, in a spirit of the love of a spouse to Christ" and, through Christ, to all of mankind.

248. One of the causes of the scarcity of vocations and of defections themselves is the fear of making final and binding decisions concerning the basic orientation of our lives.

Saint Rose and Saint Hyacintha—just as the Blessed Gabriella Sagheddu, whose mortal remains are preserved in one of your convents, that of Vitorchiano—remind us by their shining example of the need to have the strength to overcome this fear which comes from the element of uncertainty proper to our existence and to affirm with courageous humility the dignity of our being called to eternal life, and therefore to irrevocable decision. This is the way to realize truly one's human and Christian personality.

249.   In Saint Rose we see the example of this generous and total adherence to the divine call. In her short life, the heroic conviction with which she was able to welcome the Word of God into her life makes us aware of the degree and the intensity with which she lived her unconditional fidelity to God.

Admirable in this young woman is the public profession of her faith: an attitude which denotes in her that dedication to the common good of society and of the Church, which constitutes one of the essential elements of Christian love for one's neighbor, based, as we know, on listening to and doing the divine will. Indeed, it is from her intimacy with Christ the Lord and from her availability to his Spirit that Rose derived that admirable wisdom and strength which enabled her to carry out her apostolate despite the difficulties and the opposition that she encountered.

For these reasons, even in the profound changes of the times, Rose still appears today as an important reference point for all Christian girls and women who want to realize fully and with true freedom the social and ecclesial dimensions of their personality.

250.   Then, in a special way, in Saint Hyacintha we see the example of how fidelity to the divine Absolute, proper to religious consecration, always requires the mutual support which the moments of contemplation and of action must lend as parts of a sole movement, which is the path toward the Kingdom of God and progress in sanctity.

Never yield to the temptation to separate and to oppose these two moments against each other nor to emphasize one at the expense of the other, but rather seek constantly, in your thoughts and in the concreteness of daily life, to unite them closely to each other even in their necessary distinction.

The example of Saint Hyacintha is a call for all of you, dear sisters and nuns, to deepen the spiritual bonds which exist between your respective vocations—contemplative and active—with respect for and in absolute fidelity to the specific charism which the Lord has given you. A more intense exchange among you, realized in this spirit, can only perfect your religious journey and make your service to the brethren more fruitful.

The monasteries will be better able to grasp how they fit into the social and ecclesial fabric in which they live, and therefore better respond, according to their specific tasks, to the spiritual expectations of their brethren. The communities of active life, for their part, will be able to better understand how the secret of true apostolic and missionary effectiveness is found in the capacity to realize, during the course of the day, an adequate space for prayer and for intimate and filial conversation with the Lord.

251.　Here, dear sisters, are the thoughts which this happy occasion has caused to spring up in my mind. Place yourselves in the school of the saints with determination and confidence. Certainly, you must be able to grasp the substance of their teaching, beyond its transient aspects, presenting it in a language which is comprehensible to the men of today and applying it to the needs proper to our times.

With these fervent wishes, I greet you all cordially, recalling in a special way the elderly, the sick, the suffering, those who have long toiled in the Lord's vineyard. In the name of the most Blessed Virgin, to everyone goes my wish for constant progress in following Christ.

28

TO MEN AND WOMEN RELIGIOUS
IN FRIBOURG (SWITZERLAND)

June 13, 1984

252.   Praised be Jesus Christ!

His promise to be present where two or three disciples are gathered in his name (Mt 18:20) fills us with a spiritual happiness which is difficult to express. You have come here in great numbers. I thank you warmly in the name of the Lord.

Together we have directed praise and intercession to the Father, through his Son our only Mediator and Redeemer, by the inspiration of the Holy Spirit. And now I would like to comment on the exhortation made by the Apostle Paul to the Christians of Ephesus, which we heard earlier: "I implore you therefore to lead a life worthy of your vocation. Bear with one another charitably, in complete selflessness, gentleness and patience. Do all you can to preserve the unity of the Spirit by the peace that binds you together" (Eph 4:1-3).

Your Congregations and communities are concerned, I know, by the *decrease in candidates* to the religious life. This objective statement, partially explained by reasons of a socio-cultural order but also by reasons of a religious order, is not an inevitable fate, and above all must never lead you to discouragement. A renewal is possible, and, with the help of the Lord, you are able to do all that it requires. In fact, Saint Paul's encouragement to the Ephesians is for all of you an urgent call to let yourselves be convinced that a renewed vitality of your Institutes implies among other things and necessarily, a *renewal of community life*.

253.   The past has known numerous communities, with the advantages and perhaps certain burdens inherent in this style of life. Today, these same communities are

reduced in number because of advanced age and the death of their members, a decrease of entrants, and at the same time by the rise of numerous more restrictive fraternities which desire to adopt new forms of presence to the world of man (cf. Discourse to Religious in Sao Paulo, July 3, 1980).[1] At this time, it seems that a happy medium should be found or rediscovered.

To have the power to attract, a religious community must be alive and visible, composed of persons sufficiently numerous and complementary in their gifts and their functions: it is also important that it be marked by a great spirit of humble and authentic togetherness in seeking the Lord, in apostolic joys and sufferings, and reasonably open to appropriate initiatives.

254. Today's young people are not, as is too easily said, closed to the evangelical call. They can certainly move more spontaneously towards new Institutes; however, they are no less attracted to older Congregations who demonstrate vitality and remain faithful to radical and adequately presented demands. We have long had proof of this: we need only to consult the history of the Church. Often adaptations are necessary, but those possibly inspired by a relaxation or which lead to it, absolutely cannot attract the young who carry deep within themselves capabilities for radical giving, even if at times these capacities seem hesitant or blocked.

255. This renewal can be greatly helped by an active, trusting, intensified collaboration among your religious families, especially when they have the same spirit, customs and goals. The federations, associations and also the unions, already envisaged by Popes Pius XI and Pius XII, encouraged by the Council and by Pope Paul VI, following the directions given by the Decree *Perfectae Caritatis* (no. 22) and by the Motu Proprio *Ecclesiae Sanctae* (nos. 39, 40 and 41), always with respect for the freedom of individuals, can be beneficial to the life of the Church and to the Institutes themselves.

256. In any case, community life cannot survive and grow without *renunciation of self*, without humility. This is how it bears fruit, such as the purification of sensitivity, the increasing maturity of persons, the authentic development of human and spiritual qualities. In a divided world where particular interests, individual and collective selfishness, disrespect for the person and his rights often triumph, the Gospel can be made credible by the witness of true religious communities united by the Holy Spirit and living a real fraternity, thus constituting for the world a powerful sign of hope.

257. I would also like to emphasize how much the renewal of religious community life finds its source and dynamism in the *Eucharist*, "sacrament of love, sign of unity, bond of charity" (cf. Const. *Sacrosanctum Concilium*, 47). The Eucharist is the sure way to communion, that is, to union and unity with God in Christ, the sure way to the communion of all, one with another, in fraternal love. The Eucharist will make the community "one Body and one Spirit" (Eph 4:4). The Eucharist permits each member and the entire community to accomplish progressively its Passover, its passage from an existence more or less impregnated by selfishness or weakness to a life more fully given to God and to others. Dear religious, always give priority to the daily Eucharistic celebration, whether it be a question of the time reserved for the celebration or of the dignity, the recollection and the active participation which must characterize every Eucharistic celebration and edify those who occasionally attend. A religious community gives witness to its authenticity, its fervor, first of all by the manner in which it celebrates, venerates and receives the Body and Blood of the Lord.

258. This reality which is at the center of your life cannot minimize or replace other times and other forms of contact with God, which are exercises of spiritual nourishment absolutely indispensable to the life of every religious man and woman. We all know that insufficient nourishment is detrimental to physical health, and sometimes disastrous. Help one another to safeguard or to restore to its proper place the Liturgy of the Hours, personal prayer, the reading of Scripture and the Fathers, Eucharistic adoration, Marian piety which is in conformity with the teaching of the Magisterium, the monthly retreat and the regular and devout reception of the Sacrament of Reconciliation, which generates a renewed movement of conversion. Each religious family should seek to find a balance between these ways of approaching the Lord.

For those of you who, under the guidance of the Bishops, are engaged in various apostolic activities, the Eucharist and other spiritual exercises are the source of a joyful fidelity to the Lord and a dedication according to his Spirit; fidelity and dedication which inspire and enliven pastoral action in parishes, hospitals, schools or in society.

259.　And you, dear religious who have dedicated yourselves to contemplative life, draw from the Eucharist and the other forms of community and individual prayer in your monasteries the secret of your silent influence on retreatants or passing visitors. May the secret of your own happiness lie in having left everything for the Lord and in accomplishing your spiritual mission, in the name of the Church, for a humanity which lets itself be totally absorbed in difficult tasks and intense worries, as well as in the mirage of worldly goods.

260.　And you, brothers and sisters whom age or illness has forced to give up generous apostolic activities, either in your own country or in mission lands, and who feel, at least sometimes, a bit useless, be led by the Eucharist and at every moment of prayer to deepen and to live the mysterious fruitfulness of the oblation of Christ, who knew the immobility of the Cross.

Yes, may the Eucharist model your persons, fundamentally consecrated by baptism and later by religious vows, according to the *mystery of Christ Jesus* radically available to God his Father and totally given to all his brothers and sisters, especially the poorest!

261. Dear religious from all parts of Switzerland, have courage and confidence, keeping in mind the greatness and the importance of your religious vocation, for yourselves, for the Church of today and also for contemporary society!

In the Apostolic Exhortation *Redemptionis Donum* which I greatly desired to publish at the end of the recent Holy Year, I wanted to reread and ponder with religious of the whole world Jesus' words concerning a vocation, among which the following are overwhelming at least: "And looking at him, Jesus loved him" (Mk 10:21) and said to him, "if you wish to be perfect, go, sell what you have and give the money to the poor and you will have treasure in heaven; then come, follow me" (Mt 19:21). The glance and the call of Jesus are always directed to "a particular person." It is *"a love of choice"* which takes on "a spousal character." The love of Christ embraces the whole person, soul and body, whether man or woman, in that person's absolutely unique and personal "I" (cf. *Redemptionis Donum*, 3).

262. Through your personal and free response to Jesus of Nazareth, the Redeemer of the world, you have consented to abandon a way of life centered on "having" in order to commit yourselves along the narrow and magnificent paths of "being." I deeply wish and ask the Lord that each of you discover the splendor and the timeliness of your religious profession.

In its humble daily realization, it can and must be *prophetic,* in the sense that it can and must show men and women of this time what in truth builds up the human person, thanks to the search, discernment, acquisition and development of convictions and ways of being which transcend changes of time and customs.

263. Your vocation, like the Christian vocation, yet at a much more decided level, is *eschatological.*

It should help the world escape from the quicksand in which it is caught by consumer goods and a certain number of anti-values (cf. *ibid.*, nos. 4-5). Yes, the contemporary world, and especially the young, should discover through your communities and their style of life the value of a life which is poor in service of the poor, the value of a life freely committed to celibacy in order to give oneself to Christ and with him to love especially the unloved, the value of a life where obedience and fraternal community discreetly oppose the excesses of an often capricious and sterile independence.

264.   "May this witness become present everywhere and universally clear. May the people of our times, in their spiritual weariness, find in it both support and hope!...May the world of our time receive the Good News not from evangelizers who are dejected and discouraged, but from ministers of the Gospel whose lives glow with fervor, who have first received the joy of Christ!" (*Redemptionis Donum*, 16, citing *Evangelii Nuntiandi*, 80).

Having come among you as the servant of unity and truth, I pray to God who is Light, Love and Life, to breathe into your communities and fraternities a new evangelical spirit. And I confide the fervor and perseverance of each one of you to the Virgin Mary, model of the consecrated life. My prayer accompanies you always. You, too, be so good as to accompany my apostolic service with your spiritual support.

In the name of the Lord, I warmly bless you, your Institutes, your monasteries and your service of the Gospel.

---

[1] Cf. Book I—nos. 618-647.

29

TO THE BENEDICTINE COMMUNITY AND PILGRIMS, IN EINSIEDELN (SWITZERLAND)

June 15, 1984

265.　Here we are, gathered on this new morning in the shrine of Our Lady of Einsiedeln, to give praise to God. From my heart I greet the loyal guardians of this place of grace, the sons of Saint Benedict and their entire monastic community. I greet those who have come on pilgrimage here today, as well as all those who are joining in the celebration of this divine service at home with their families.

　　We sang just now in our first psalm: "O God, you are my God whom I seek. . .for you my soul thirsts. Thus have I gazed toward you in the sanctuary, to see your power and your glory" (Ps 62:2,3). The voice of that psalm is our voice: "God, you are my God. . ." This yearning to see God is rooted in every human heart—although it is often stifled: yearning for an everlastingly happy fullness of life, yearning for God. If our inner voice does not become drowned, we hear our hearts calling for an experience of God. The psalmist's words come again and again to our lips: "God, you are my God. . .my soul thirsts for you. . ." We seek a happiness that can be found only in him.

266.　But God does not let himself be experienced in the way that things of nature are experienced. That is why, like the psalmist, we watch for him in his "holy place." We can meet God only in faith. Isaiah speaks in today's reading of his own personal experience of God. He looked in a hidden way upon the holy God and heard the song of praise: "Holy, holy, holy is the Lord" (Is 6:3). As a man, he experienced the holy awe-inspiring God and his own sinfulness at the same time: "woe is me." The experience of the nearness of God is a borderline experience for man. But the prophet also heard the forgiving words: "Your guilt is blotted out" (*ibid.*, 6:5-7). The nearness of the holy God is a loving and healing nearness, an experience which makes one happy: when God calls to his presence, he saves.

267.   This morning, like the psalmist, we are watching together for God in Mary's holy place. Even more than the Prophet Isaiah, Mary experienced what it means to be near God. Mary is the virgin whose heart is not divided: she cares only for the things of the Lord and will please him alone in her deeds and thoughts (cf. 1 Cor 7:32-34). At the same time, however, she too feels a holy fear of God and "was troubled" by the words of God's message. God had picked this maiden out, and he sanctified her as the dwelling place of his Word.

Mary, the lofty daughter of Sion, experienced more than anyone else how near God's "power and glory" are. She uttered a cry of full and thankful joy in the Magnificat: "My being proclaims the greatness of the Lord...God who is mighty has done great things for me. Holy is his name." Mary was at the same time deeply aware of her state of being a creature: "He has looked upon his servant in her lowliness." She knew that all peoples would call her blessed (cf. Lk 1:46-49), but she herself pointed to Jesus: "Do what he tells you" (Jn 2:5). She concerns herself with the things of the Lord. In her ever-renewed readiness for her God, Mary "advanced in her pilgrimage of faith" (*Lumen Gentium,* 58). The maiden of Nazareth looked upon God's incomprehensible dealings with the eyes of faith. Luke emphasized twice that she reflected "in her heart" on what had happened to her (Lk 2: 19,51). Such faith is prized and declared blessed: "Blessed is she who has believed..." (cf. Lk 1:45).

268.   Dear brothers and sisters: follow the pilgrim path of faith which Mary followed. Like her, open up your hearts entirely to the things of the Lord. I direct this call to all: to bishops, priests and deacons, to religious and laity, men and women. In all of us lives a human being's yearning for the experience of the living God. This yearning

has again and again called men and women to the way of faithfully following Christ. Is not this shrine of Mary imbued with the yearning of innumerable pilgrims in faith looking for God's presence in this world? Here such seekers have been able to enter into an atmosphere of prayer. In this place the holy hermit Meinrad (d. 861) sought God in stillness. Numerous saints made pilgrimages here: Bishops Ulrich (d. 983), Wolfgang (d. 994), and Konrad (d. 995), Dorothea of Montau (about 1384), the man of prayer Nicholas of Flue (about 1474), that renewer of Church life, Charles Borromeo (1570), the catechist Peter Canisius (d. 1597), Brother Benedict Joseph Labre (d. 1783), the helper of the poor, Jeanne Antida Thouret (1795) and so many other nameless saints. They and all pilgrims were conscious of their need for help and of their sinfulness. They lingered in prayer here with Mary, open to God and his Spirit.

269.   So is the faith carried on: the living faith of prayer, of personal acquaintance with God. Whoever seeks the community of believers, whoever especially draws near to Mary, enters into an atmosphere of the Spirit. Mary already accepted the offer of grace and of the Spirit (cf. Lk 1:28,35). Like Mary, let us be open to God's Spirit, so that we may experience his power, which renders us fit for the service and testimony to which we are called.

270.   Dear brothers and sisters: concern yourselves with the things of the Lord, keep watch for the holy God. I once again recall the Prophet Isaiah's vision of his calling. His mission to mankind was rooted in his personal experience of the thrice-holy God. He then became ready to hear the voice of the Lord. He understood the call to dispose himself to prophetic service, and he gave his consent to being sent from on high: "Here am I, send me" (Is 6:8). Now he had the commission: "Go and say to this people, you must hear. . ." (cf. Is 6:9). The prophet was taken into service by God without conditions. He thenceforth stood undividedly on God's side. But he was also to remain solidly with the people to whom he was sent.

271.   Mary too had been able at once to experience the presence of the Lord: "The Lord is with you." She accepted the offer of grace before she wondered about her fitness for that singular mission to become Mother of the Messiah. Thus she gave her unreserved "yes" to cooperation with God's work of salvation: "I am the servant of the Lord. Let it be done to me as you say" (Lk 1:38). She acted with reflection, but she did not set any conditions. She was ready for service, for she knew that she was near the holy God. In humility she went "the pilgrim way of faith," to the foot of her Son's Cross. She is wholly with us on that way: a sympathetic mother and sister.

272.   Let us, dear brothers and sisters, take Mary, Jesus' Mother, who is also the Church's and our mother, as our model and our companion on the way of our earthly pilgrimage. In all situations of our lives, let us watch with her for the holy God, who is ever other and greater than we, who is nonetheless ever in a mysterious way with us and who loves us. In the sight of this God, who became our Father in Christ, let us also say, "Here am I, send me." "Be it done to me as you say," in the service of God and of human beings. Amen.

30

TO THE GENERAL CHAPTER OF THE MISSIONARY CONGREGATION OF THE HANDMAIDS OF THE HOLY SPIRIT

July 7, 1984

273.   With great happiness I receive you in this audience especially reserved for you, and I offer my greetings to you here present, who have participated in the ninth General Chapter Meeting of your Congregation, and through you to all your fellow sisters, who, numbering four thousand, carry out their missionary commitment in twenty-six nations on five continents.

For two months you have been working and praying intensely to work out your Constitutions in a definitive form and to elect your new representatives, and I wish to express to you my heartfelt participation in your desire for structural renewal while maintaining the direction of the charism of your foundation, and for a deeper spiritual fervor, so especially necessary in today's world. I wish from my heart for your Congregation an abundance of the fruits of the Holy Spirit (cf. Gal 5:22-23) in order to be in every place a constant praise to God, an example to the brethren, and an instrument of salvation and sanctification.

I desire especially that your Congregation, which for so many years has labored untiringly for the proclamation of the Gospel and the spreading of the Kingdom of God among souls, may persevere with constancy and fervor in the mission you have undertaken, open to the needs of the contemporary world, not fearing adversity and difficulties, receiving every needy brother and sister with love, invoking unceasingly the light and the joy of the Holy Spirit, always mindful of what the Second Vatican Council says: "the Church both works and prays, that all of mankind may become the People of God, the Mystical Body of Christ, the

Temple of the Holy Spirit, and that in Christ, the center of all things, all honor and glory may be rendered to the Creator and Father of the universe" (*Lumen Gentium,* 17b).

274.　Your missionary commitment also takes on a particular physiognomy and mark as a result of the special charism of your Congregation of Religious "Handmaids of the Holy Spirit." It is a title of great honor, but also of great responsibility! You are at the service of the mystery of divine love!

In regard to the concrete reality of your special charism, you are first of all in the service of the Truth, because the Holy Spirit is Truth. Let us recall the words of Jesus: "When the Paraclete comes, the Spirit of truth who comes from the Father—and whom I myself will send from the Father—he will bear witness on my behalf. You must bear witness as well" (Jn 15:26-27).

Jesus speaks elsewhere, in an impressive way, of this Spirit of Truth (cf. Jn 14:16 ff. and 16:13 ff.), and his words are of unique and fundamental importance because they assure us that he has revealed the saving truth which comes from the Father himself, and he has guaranteed its permanence and necessary development through the Holy Spirit, entrusting it to the Church founded on Peter and the Apostles.

Let your first commitment be, therefore, to serve the Spirit of Truth, remaining closely united to the authentic and perennial Magisterium of the Church, which carries forward in time the illuminating and salvific message of Christ.

275.　I said recently during my apostolic journey to Switzerland that "even if the world around us doubts the presence of a God who loves it, the ability of Christ to renew it, and the power of the Holy Spirit who continues his work of sanctification, even if the world does not feel the need to accept such a salvation and seems to count only on its technical capacities or to reduce its horizon to a materialistic life, the Church maintains the conviction that there is no other name outside that of Christ that can save mankind: he is the Way, the Truth, and the Life" (Speech to the representatives of the Swiss clergy—Einsiedeln, June 15, 1984). Saint Augustine admonished: "Each one possesses the Holy Spirit in proportion to his love for the Church of God" (In Joh. Tract. 32:8).

276. In the second place you must sense that you are in the service of the Spirit the Comforter. Certainly it is necessary to "suffer with him who suffers" (cf. Rm 12:15), to combat evil and social injustice, and to promote civil progress, but without ever forgetting and living the gifts of the Holy Spirit, which are in us by means of sanctifying grace and the sacramental graces. The true, authentic, profound, and lasting consolations are those that proceed from the Holy Spirit and make us enjoy the presence of God in ourselves, enlighten us about the eschatological perspective of existence and all of human history, help us accept the mysterious but saving plan of Providence, commit us to the struggle against sin and the demands of asceticism, and let us taste Eucharistic intimacy with Christ and the joy of prayer. The Holy Spirit consoles us with divine Wisdom: therefore consider yourselves in his service in your missionary labors!

277. Finally, we know that the Holy Spirit is the love that proceeds from the Father and the Son: the reciprocal love of the Father and of the Son is a Person subsisting of himself in the unique divine nature, and he is the first and last motive of all creation and of the redemption of humanity. We are all, therefore, in the service of divine love, but for you, who are the "Handmaids of Love" because you are consecrated to the Holy Spirit, there lies open an immense field of labor and apostolate, which finds its clearest definition in the fruits of the Spirit enumerated, as you know, by Saint Paul: "love, joy, peace, patience, benevolence, goodness, fidelity, meekness, and self-control" (Gal 5:22-23). Walk therefore according to the Spirit, even if perhaps the road is tiresome and difficult, because, as the Apostle adds,

"those who belong to Christ Jesus have crucified their flesh with its passions and desires" (*ibid.,* 5:24).

278.   May the Virgin Mary, who was totally sanctified by the Holy Spirit, make you always feel the joy of the "soul's sweet Guest," make you always open to his inspirations, and keep you always burning with enthusiasm to be handmaids of infinite and merciful Love! And may my Apostolic Blessing, which I cordially impart, accompany you and your entire Congregation.

31

TO THE CANONS REGULAR OF
SAINT AUGUSTINE, IN ROME

July 10, 1984

279.   It is a great joy for me to welcome you here in the Vatican, especially your Abbot Primate (for whose deferential words I am grateful), the Abbots General of the Congregations—including the Superior General of the Congregation of the Immaculate Conception—and the other Abbots. A particular reason has drawn you to come together in Rome from the various parts of the earth to hold a Congress: namely, that it was in this city, twenty-five years ago, that you entered into the Confederation, in the Lateran Basilica, which your Order served for such a long time. The intention of this Confederation is that the parts of your Order "be united among themselves by the bond of love, increase the strength of the entire Order, and help each other, especially as regards spirituality, the education of the young, and culture" (Apostolic Brief "Caritatis Unitas," May 4, 1959; *AAS* 51, [1959], p. 631).

280.   I have known your Order very well for a long time, through the Lateran Congregation of the Most Holy Redeemer, since it has the principal house of its Polish Province at Krakow and labors in the Lord's vineyard in various places in my native land. It is an exceedingly ancient Order, wholly clerical, in that it binds together the religious life in fraternal community with the liturgical and pastoral ministry. In this, you have the glorious example of Saint Augustine, whose Rule you follow, and who "wished to have in the bishop's house a monastery of clerics" (cf. Sermon 355, 1; PL 39, 1570).

281.   A great deal is said in our age about the identity
       of religious families, in a period when men are ex-
posed to rapid change and new psychological factors
emerge, especially among the young, and too much weight
perhaps is attached to external activity. You too, accord-
ingly, must give diligent consideration to your true identity. Since "it is for the good of the Church that the religious
Institutes should have their own character and task" (*Perfectae Caritatis,* 2), you must endeavor with care to maintain the place which Divine Providence has assigned to you
in the Church, providing where necessary for new needs,
and not departing from traditions of proved worth.

282.   As canons, you are bound to the solemn divine wor-
       ship in your churches, a worship that consists above
all in the choral celebration of the Liturgy of the Hours
and the Eucharist. Mindful that "the liturgy is the summit to which the action of the Church tends, and at the
same time the spring from which all her strength flows"
(cf. *Sacrosanctum Concilium,* 10), you must strive with fresh
vigor of soul to fulfill worthily and fruitfully this duty,
which is peculiarly yours and is laid upon you by the
Church. In this area, a special form of the apostolate is
yours, as priests with the care of souls: you are to lead the
faithful "to the conscious and active participation in the
liturgical celebrations" (*ibid.*, 14), especially to take part
with you in at least some part of the Liturgy of the Hours.

283.   It is necessary that the liturgical celebration be
       joined to personal prayer, for the Lord teaches that
we must pray to the Father in secret (cf. Mt 6:6) and Saint
Paul charges us to pray without ceasing (cf. 1 Thess 5:17).
It is no small struggle that is needed, if one is to lead a
life joined as closely as possible to God amid so much
worldly clamor, so much agitation of humankind, so many
things that easily distract the mind from "the one thing
needful" (cf. Lk 10:42). Here the following words of Saint
Augustine are apt: "The sound of the external voices is
heard for a time, then is silent—but the sound of the inter-
nal voice must be continuous. When you come to church

to sing a hymn, your voice sounds forth the praises of God; you have said as much as you could, you have departed; but let your soul continue to sound forth the praises of God" (Commentary on Ps 102:2; PL 37, 1317). It is obvious that this spiritual nourishment of personal piety is related to the pastoral ministry also. Take as your example that luminary of your Order, Alan de Solminihac, who was beatified nearly three years ago: he indeed made the liturgical life and an extremely taxing apostolic activity fruitful by the practice of prayer.

284.   You are called canons *regular* because of the reform of the ancient institution of the canons, with the restoration of the common life without private property at the Lateran Synod in 1059. Rightly do we read in the Declaration on the Canonical Life, which you wrote jointly after the Second Vatican Council: "The common life, which is one of the chief characteristics of the Order... gives the families of canons strength to carry out the ministries better and thus to acquire the perfection of charity, fulfills the personality of each one, and safeguards from dangers."

285.   Let each one of the communities of canons regular, therefore, be "a true family, gathered together in the Lord" (*Perfectae Caritatis,* 15), in which there flourishes the communion of hearts, in that the members "live as one in the house, having one heart and one mind set upon God" (cf. Rule of Saint Augustine, 1); in which there flourishes the communion of prayer, to which they "apply themselves at the appointed times and seasons" (cf. *ibid.,* 3); in which there flourishes the communion of actions, whereby "their works are done together" (*ibid.,* 8), especially as regards pastoral activity; in which there flourishes the communion of goods, so that they have "all things in common" (cf. *ibid.,* 1). From such a community a "great apostolic strength flows forth," as the Second Vatican Council declares in a passage that deserves close attention (*Perfectae Caritatis,* 15).

286. The celebration of the silver jubilee of the foundation of your Confederation is a point at which you
must pause and give very close consideration to what it
means: this union of your Congregations, founded above
all on charity, is entirely appropriate in our times, when
relations between men are more rapid and their will to
work jointly is more keen. The Confederation should not
be merely a name without a reality. It is necessary that
it be constantly vitalized and filled with the spirit of true
fraternity and cooperation; thus it will respond to the expectation of the Church which approved it.

Be sincere and faithful sons of this Church. Hear
once more Saint Augustine, your father and lawgiver: "Let
us love the Lord our God, let us love his Church: him as
our Father, her as our Mother; him as the Lord, her as his
handmaid; for we are the sons of the handmaid herself. . .With one mind then, beloved, hold to God the Father
and to the Church the Mother" (Commentary on Ps 88:14;
PL 37, 1140-1141).

287. The best figure of this Church is the Blessed Virgin
Mary, to whose Immaculate Heart your Order is consecrated. Imitate Mary, who was always wholly submissive
to the will of God! Obey her when she urges you, speaking
of her Son: "Whatever he says to you, do" (Jn 2:5).

Finally, to strengthen and confirm you, so that you
may zealously accomplish your noble vocation, I gladly impart to all of you who are present here the Apostolic Blessing, which I wish to extend also to your individual religious
families, the canonesses regular and the other sisters who
follow the ideals of your Order, and to the *familiares,* that
is, to the diocesan priests and laity who are joined by
spiritual bonds to your Institute.

32

TO PRIESTS AND MEN AND WOMEN RELIGIOUS IN FANO (ITALY)

August 12, 1984

288. I feel a deep desire to express to you cordially my joy and my satisfaction for this meeting. Joy, because it allows me to enter into immediate harmony with you by reason of ideals, of hopes, of choices, in a word, of the vocation which, by providential divine disposition, unites us all. Satisfaction, because I see in you, coming from Fano, Fossombrone, Cagli and Pergola, the sign of unity among the four diocesan communities. Led by Msgr. Costanzo Micci and supported by your pastoral charity, they walk together and gather today around the Successor of Peter, in order to grow in the communion which confirms the presence of Christ in the world.

With you who, as priests and consecrated persons, have decided to dedicate your life to the service of God, preferring nothing to the love of Christ, walking with a free and fervent heart on the path of the Lord, I want to meditate today on the greatness of the gift of the priesthood and on the total gift of oneself in religious life, which witness that it is God who gives life its full meaning.

289. First of all, I address you, beloved priests, inviting you to thank the immense divine goodness that has called you to the priesthood for the service of the Church and of mankind.

The priest is the minister of Christ, chosen by him and consecrated to him, a witness of his Passion, death and Resurrection, sent by him to communicate the divine life of grace, especially through Eucharistic worship and the celebration of the sacraments.

The priest has the mission to be teacher and guide, because he must preach the Gospel and give an answer to the endless questions of man, of every man, about the ultimate meaning of created reality.

The priest, then, being in the world as a sign and witness of Christ's salvific love, and officially deputed to the public prayer of the Church, continually offers to God that sacrifice of praise (cf. Heb 13:15) that expresses the groaning of all creation toward the freedom of the sons of God (cf. Rom 8:19); and, in this way, he becomes their mediator and spokesman.

290. Our duty as priests is then that of *witnessing to the faith,* exercising the *"kingly office."* As had been stressed by Vatican Council II, the kingly mission of Jesus Christ is transmitted in a special way to the Church under the form of pastoral power, which the bishops exercise in communion with the Successor of Peter, and which the priests and deacons exercise under the direction of the bishops (cf. *Lumen Gentium,* 18ff.). Such pastoral power has its origin, its continuous raison d'etre, its model and ideal in Christ, the Good Shepherd, who gives his life for his sheep (cf. Jn 10:15), and, when he finds that which is lost, puts it on his shoulders in jubilation (cf. Lk 15:5).

291. To witness to the faith as priests is, therefore, to sanctify oneself and to serve Christ in others with that *pastoral charity* which, lived in communion, makes priests perfect in unity (cf. Jn 17:23), and heralds of the Son of God, the Savior: "Father, that they may all be one so that the world may believe" (Jn 17:21).

To witness to the faith as priests is *to give oneself generously to the "ministry of the Word,"* seeking the most fitting way to proclaim the Gospel to "every creature" (Mk 16:15), carefully assuring that an appropriate catechesis, developed in an organic, synthetic and profound manner, reaches all types of people, especially young people, who are sometimes left without any help.

292. To witness to the faith as priests *is to be channels of grace,* in order to communicate divine life through the worthy celebration of the divine mysteries, the adminis-

tration of the sacraments and especially the Sacrament of Reconciliation, and to lead the faithful to the love of the good, the ultimate source of correct moral judgments.

To witness to the faith as priests is to make oneself *totally available to God* so that "he may make of us an everlasting gift to him" (cf. Eucharistic Prayer III). Thus, we speak to the Lord, to our Creator and Father, in the name and in the person of Christ, and at the same time, in the name of all creatures, so as to be always truly *men-for:* for God and for the brethren, without reserve, in the complete joy of the gift of self.

To witness to the faith as priests is, finally, to be *men of prayer,* partakers in a special way in the prayer of Jesus: men of God, consecrated, we lend our voices, at the peak moments of each day, to the same Christ who praises the Father and continually intercedes for us (cf. Heb 7:25).

293.   I wish, then, to encourage you to persevere with confidence and with fervor in your noble priestly and pastoral mission, in mutual charity and in unity of purpose. Today's world especially needs enlightened and sound guides. I repeat also to you what I said to the priests of Switzerland: "The more unchristian the world becomes, the more it needs to see in the person of priests that radical faith, which is like a beacon in the night, or the rock upon which it is supported."[1] We must live as brothers with the men of our times, while always remaining "witnesses and dispensers of a life different from the earthly one" (*Presbyterorum Ordinis,* 3).

294.   You, too, dear brothers and sisters, who have made a privileged covenant with Christ, Redeemer of man and of the world, by the profession of the evangelical counsels: continue faithfully to call upon God, to pray, in order to persevere on the road to which he has called you. Prayer is the strength of the weak. The Apostle Paul says: "The Spirit too helps us in our weakness, for we do not know how to pray as we ought; but the Spirit himself makes intercession for us with groanings that cannot be expressed in speech" (Rom 8:26).

Prayer enables us in a certain sense to live in the dimension of God, to enter, in a humble but courageous way, into the very heart of God, into his plan. To pray is to acknowledge that Christ is risen and deserves our unconditional dedication.

295.   But if your way of life makes evident the primacy of contemplation, which, articulated and supported by your Rule, increases your love for Christ, it is no less evident that this love constitutes a special good for the whole Church. The People of God are aware that, in the love which Christ receives from consecrated persons, the love of the entire Body is directed in a special way toward the Spouse.

296.   I express to you the gratitude of the Church for your consecration and your profession of the evangelical counsels, which are a characteristic witness of love, through which the whole redemptive truth of the Gospel becomes especially visible. I exhort you, therefore, to participate in the Church's apostolate according to the specific charism of the Order or Congregation in which you live. I hope, therefore, that you will always be open to the pastoral life of the local Church and that, attentive to the signs of the times, you will always be generously available to respond to the needs of the poor, in order to bring Christ's message to those most in need of concrete signs of the Redeemer's salvific hope. Many are the ways in which, through the apostolate, you can and must manifest your love for the Church and for the world. Nevertheless, the important thing is that, both in contemplation, which is fruitful for the proclamation of Christ, and in action directly apostolic, you be a living proof that "the Kingdom of God is not a matter of eating or drinking, but of justice, peace, and the joy that is given by the Holy Spirit. Whoever serves Christ in this way pleases God and wins the esteem of men" (Rom 14:17-18). The world has need of the authentic witness of religious consecration as a constant yeast of saving renewal.

196

297. I wish to conclude by reminding you that the purpose of religious life is to honor and glorify the Blessed Trinity and, through your consecration, to help mankind reach the fullness of life in the Father, Son and Holy Spirit. In all your projects and in all your activities, seek to have this aim always before you. You will not be able to render a greater service; you will not be able to receive a greater reward.

Along with my wish that the Lord and the Virgin Mary, our gentle Mother, accompany you, dear priests, dear men and women religious, and fill your life with great enthusiasm in the service of your high calling and your ecclesial ministry, with all my heart I impart to you all my Apostolic Blessing.

---

[1] Cf. L'Osservatore Romano, July 23, 1984, p. 10.

33

TO THE BENEDICTINES OF THE MOST BLESSED SACRAMENT IN ALATRI (ITALY)

September 2, 1984

298. I want to express to you, dear sisters, my joy on this visit to Alatri. I have been invited to celebrate the fourth centenary of the discovery of the mortal remains of Saint Sixtus I, Pope and Martyr, who was one of the first successors to the See of Peter in Rome. We are all familiar with Saint Sixtus because his name is mentioned in the first Eucharistic Prayer, the Roman Canon, after that of Clement. He lived at the time of the emperor Adrian, at the beginning of the second century after Christ.

299. I am deeply moved by this visit which takes us back to an era so ancient and at the same time so near. When we realize that here, as in all chapels, we find ourselves in the presence of the most Blessed Sacrament, which is the same divine food which nourished the first Christians, then we begin to see the Church in both its historical and mystical dimensions.

It is a mystery that, during so many centuries, so many generations, the same Body has nourished and continues to nourish such a great number of persons: faithful, witnesses, confessors, martyrs. Even more, the same Body, the Eucharistic Body of Christ, makes of us one Body, because the Church is the Body of Christ. This has been reaffirmed time and time again; Pope Pius XII taught it in his encyclical *Mystici Corporis,* and the Pauline tradition clearly affirms it. And here, dear sisters, in this Mystical Body of Christ, you have a special part, a privileged part. But this privilege costs dearly; it requires sacrifice, the sacrifice of your lives entirely consecrated to the Lord, without reserve. And this is the privilege of each one of you, a noble vocation by which the Church can live, always more intensely, the gift of the Redemption. You will recall that with these words, *"Redemptionis donum,"* I began a special letter which I addressed to all the men and women religious in the Church on the occasion of the Holy Year of the Redemption.

300.   This encounter gives me great joy. I am happy to be among you, in your enclosure, here where you pray, where the Eucharistic Christ is adored, night and day, glorified in your hearts, in your words, in your sentiments, and in your souls. I join you in this adoration, in this prayer, which is that of the whole Church throughout the world. In your prayers, in your hearts, I would even say in your hands, you bear the lot and the destiny of the Church and of the world.

I recommend myself and the entire Church to your prayers, to your total consecration to the Lord, to your contemplative vocation as Benedictines. I say this to you here present, and also to all the other contemplative religious, first to those of your Federation and those who follow your Benedictine Rule, then to all the contemplative sisters in the world, whatever their rule and Constitutions. And I say it also, having before my eyes this image of the Virgin Mother of Jesus, and Mother of the Church.

With my Apostolic Blessing.

34

TO WOMEN RELIGIOUS IN HULL, PROVINCE OF QUEBEC (CANADA)

September 19, 1984

301. "The Spirit and the Bride say 'Come'. . . Come, Lord Jesus" (Rev 22:17, 20). The Church, inspired by the Spirit present in it, continues to address this call to the Lord Jesus. She awaits his return. The Church awaits him, as a bride yearning after her beloved husband who is at the right hand of the Father. She has already "washed her robes" in his redeeming Blood. She hopes "to feed on the tree of life." She knows that she already shares in his life in a mysterious and partial way, through faith, the sacraments, prayer and charity. It is with him that she works to renew this world according to his Spirit. But she is impatient for a complete renewal, for the full vision of her Spouse. For the moment, her life is hidden in God.

The whole Church must live in this expectancy and bear witness to it. But consecrated souls have made "a charismatic choice of Christ as the exclusive Spouse." This choice already enables one "to be anxious about the affairs of the Lord" but also—when it is made "for the Kingdom of heaven"—it brings this eschatological reign of God closer to the life of all people. Consecrated persons bring into the midst of this passing world news of the resurrection to come and of eternal life (cf. my letter *Redemptionis Donum*, 11).

302. All religious men and women have this charism at the heart of the Church. But it is even more obvious in the case of cloistered sisters who give up all activity in the world in order to be present to the Lord alone. And in this place it is first of all to you that I speak, dear contemplative sisters. The Church considers your place in the Mystical Body of Christ essential to the life of the Church, to its full development, and this, even in the young Churches

whose energy is monopolized by the tasks of evangelization (cf. *Perfectae Caritatis,* 7, and *Ad Gentes,* 40). In fact, the prayer of contemplatives has played a considerable role in the deepening of faith in Canada. That was certainly the insight of Father Mangin and Sister Marie-Zita de Jesus when they founded here, almost a hundred years ago, the Servants of Jesus and Mary. These religious women honor in a special way the Sacred Heart of Jesus in the Eucharist, the supreme gift of his love, before which they keep a continuous vigil. Is not your spiritual apostolate, dear sisters, to support the ministry of priests and to collaborate in the eternal plan of the covenant for all believers: "that they might be one"? I think also of all the men and women who have established the contemplative life in Canada according to complementary spiritualities. So, in addition to all the religious here today, I greet with affection and I encourage all those who lead a monastic life in Canada!

"The Kingdom of heaven will be like this: ten bridesmaids took their lamps and went to meet the bridegroom. Five of them were foolish and five were wise." My sisters, wait for the Groom as these wise virgins did. Always be ready. Always be open. In your waiting for the Lord, keep watch.

303.   Your convent life is organized in such a way as to encourage the experience of God. Your withdrawal from the world, with its solitude; your silence, which is a listening silence, a silence of love; asceticism, penance, the tasks which lead you to share in the redemptive work; fraternal communion which is always being renewed; the daily Eucharistic celebration that unites your offering to that of Christ.

May the weariness, routine and monotony involved in your convent life not make you lose your vigilance; may the occasional impression that God is absent or temptations or even the normal trials of growing in mystical union with Christ not discourage you! May the lamp of your prayer, of your love, never stop burning! Keep it well supplied with oil, day and night.

304. For, even within a community, your path is still a personal one. Just as the wise virgins were incapable of making up for the carelessness of the foolish virgins, no one else can take your place in welcoming the Trinitarian life into the depth of yourself, where the love received responds in adoration, praise and gratitude to love. It is then that you make your own the prayer of the psalmist we were reading a moment ago: "God, you are my God, I am seeking you, my soul is thirsting for you, my flesh is longing for you, a land parched, weary and waterless; I long to gaze on you in the sanctuary and to see your power and glory. Your love is better than life itself. . .all my life I will bless you. . .I meditate on you all night long. . .I sing for joy in the shadow of your wings. My soul clings close to you, your right hand supports me" (Ps 63 [62]:2-5, 7-9).

305. This ineffable meeting with the personal and living God can take place only in the darkness of faith. The Groom stands behind the door while you are still outside in the night. It is always in the light of faith that God gives himself. But the signs of God are so discreet in the ordinariness of your everyday life that you must be vigilant if you are to persevere and grow in faith in imitation of Mary. The "treasure" that awaits you in heaven will only be the eschatological fulfillment of what is hidden in the inner "treasure" of the heart (cf. *Redemptionis Donum,* 5).

306. Your lives have a hidden but assured fruitfulness. "Whoever remains in me. . .bears fruit in plenty" (Jn 15:5). In the solidarity that unites all the members of Christ, you are like the heart, as Saint Theresa of the Child Jesus put it. Without your love, charity would grow cold. In the Church that prays, suffers and evangelizes, your part is the relationship with God. Your offering makes you like Christ so that he can use your whole being for the work of redemption according to the pleasure of his love. And God hears the prayer of praise and intercession that rises up from your hearts and dispenses his grace, without which there would be neither conversion to the Gospel, growth

in faith nor vocations of apostolic workers in the Church (cf. Decree *Ad Gentes,* 40).

The Christian community in Hull seems to have clearly understood your vocation, as has the neighboring community of the city of Ottawa. People are attached to your monastery and support it. They do not hesitate to entrust you with their sorrows and their joys, their plans and their prayer intentions.

307.　More and more people—and among them, many young people—are seeking places of grace, of prayer, of contemplation. They are thirsting for the absolute. Some come to your monasteries in search of spiritual values. To all these seekers after God, show by the truth and the transparency of your persons that belonging to Christ makes you free and that the experience of God fulfills you. Without shirking the requirements of contemplative life, find ways of expressing for the culture of our time your radical option for God. To those who say: "We do not know how to pray," say again and again by your existence that dialogue with God is possible for "the Spirit too comes to help us in our weakness" (Rom 8:26). To those who want to do something great with their life, testify that the path to holiness is the most beautiful of adventures. It is not just the work of our efforts, but that of the infinite tenderness of God in the vastness of human misery. May your monasteries allow passers-by to approach the sources of living water: "Then let all who are thirsty come: all who want it may have the water of life and have it free" (Rev 22:17)!

308.　My meditation has seemed to be focused on cloistered nuns. But, all along, I have had in mind all the women who have devoted themselves to God in religious life in Canada. There are almost forty thousand of them! What I said about the spirit of consecrated life is also valid for all the sisters dedicated to an active or apostolic life. Circumstances have not permitted a special meeting with them as a group, and I regret that. I have seen many of them at every stage of my visit, with the People of God. But I was waiting for this opportunity and now, this evening, I am happy to greet them all from this place of contemplation and to address to them this message.

Dear sisters, in the Church, you carry out services that are precious to Christian communities and to the world: among other things, you are involved in teaching catechism, in education, in hospital care, in supporting the elderly and in parish activities. . . Happy are the villages and the cities where sisters are still present! You exercise a certain professional activity, with preference for activity which allows you to express charity and to give witness to faith, and that, in a community way.

309. But that is not the original mystery of your life. You freely consecrated yourself to the Lord who was the first to choose you. Your religious vows are intimately rooted in the consecration of baptism but express it with greater fullness (cf. *Perfectae Caritatis,* 5). You share in a special and permanent way in the Redeemer's death on the Cross and in his Resurrection. The Paschal nature of your life is evident in each of the "evangelical counsels" which you have committed yourselves to practice in a radical way. At the same time you become truly free in order better to serve. You stake your all, not on "having" but on the quality of "being," the quality of the person renewed in Jesus Christ!

More than ever before, our world needs to discover in your communities and in your lifestyle the value of a simple and poor life in the service of the poor, the value of a life freely committed in celibacy in order to consecrate itself to Christ and, with him, to love especially those deprived of love, the value of a life where obedience and community life silently protest the excesses of an independence that is sometimes irresponsible and barren.

310. Above all, the world needs witnesses of the free gift of the love of God. To those who doubt the existence of God, or who have the impression that he is absent, you show that the Lord is worth seeking and loving for himself; that the Kingdom of God, despite its apparent

foolishness, is worth devoting one's life to. Thus, your lives are a sign of the indestructible faith of the Church. The free giving of your life to Christ and to others is perhaps the protest that most urgently needs to be made to a society where profit-making efficiency has become an idol. Your choice amazes, questions, interests or irritates the world, but it never leaves it indifferent. In any case, the Gospel is always the sign of contradiction. You will not be understood by all. But never be afraid to manifest your consecration to the Lord. It is your honor! It is an honor to the Church! You have a special place in the Body of Christ where everyone has his or her role to assume, his or her own charism.

If, with the Holy Spirit, you seek the holiness which corresponds to your state of life, do not be afraid. He will not abandon you. Vocations will come to you, and you will keep your youthfulness of soul, which has nothing to do with age. Yes, my dear sisters, live in hope. Keep your eyes on Christ and walk firmly in his footsteps in joy and in peace.

35

TO THE ABBOTS AND CONVENTUAL PRIORS
OF THE BENEDICTINE FEDERATION, IN ROME

September 27, 1984

311. I am very happy to meet you, to greet you in the Lord
with all my affection, and to profit of this occasion
to encourage you to follow the Benedictine Rule with con-
scientiousness and firmness, to renew your lifestyle, to
reflect on your works and your institutions. I know that
you are taking part in the General Congress of the Benedictine Federation at the Monastery of Saint Anselm, on the
Aventin. I know, also, that with a great consensus and an
enthusiastic agreement, you have confirmed the Reverend
Father Victor Dammertz in his office of Abbot Primate. I
offer him my congratulations and promise him my prayers
for a fruitful accomplishment of his office and a peaceful
government of the Benedictine family, according to the
norms of your federation. You have thus come here this
morning in order to "see Peter" and perhaps also to receive
from him a fraternal word, which may remain with you as
a remembrance of your Congress in Rome and of your meeting with the Vicar of Christ.

312. I do not want to detain you here too long, nor speak
to you at too great a length. Nevertheless, the title
of your Congress suggests to me some typically Benedictine reflections. "And you, who do you say that I am?" (Mk
8:29). It is certainly a question, in the first place, of a
knowledge of Christ and an intimacy with him, then of a
witness to be given to Christ among men today. Today still,
Christ asks men what they think of him, or better yet, what
you yourselves think of him. Your life is a following of
Christ: you follow him, because you know who he is. People will come to you in order to learn, to experience, to see
who Jesus Christ is, from the example of your life, your

liturgical rites, the fruits of your works. Your monasteries are the place where you yourselves have come to know Jesus of Nazareth, where he lives with you always, as guest and companion. Your monasteries will therefore also be the place where the men and women of our time will come to search for the signs of the presence of Christ, of the brotherhood of Christ, of the charity of Christ, of the holiness of Christ.

313.   Rather than speak of your life with Christ, it would be more exact and truer to speak of the life of Christ with you. Then, when you encounter difficulties along the way, you are consoled by his assurance: "Courage, it is I, do not be afraid!" (Mk 6:50). He is your companion and guide, your food and drink, your rod and your staff (Ps 23). It is of your daily journeying with Christ that the Conciliar decree *Perfectae Caritatis* (no. 5) speaks: "Therefore, in fidelity to their profession and in renunciation of all things for the sake of Christ (cf. Mk 10:28), let religious follow him (cf. Mt 19:21) as their one necessity (cf. Lk 10:42). Let them listen to his words (cf.Lk 10:39) and be preoccupied with his work" (cf. 1 Cor 7:32).

314.   You, Benedictines, travel this road with Christ "in the school of the service of the Lord" as the Rule of Saint Benedict (Prol. 45) clearly states. This school offers you a continual teaching, given by the Holy Spirit, listening to the words of the Teacher (cf. *Rule,* Prol. 1) who is Christ. The "lectio divina" provides you with a wonderfully efficacious aide for acquiring "the excelling knowledge of Jesus Christ" (Phil 3:8, *Dei Verbum,* 25). At the same time, this school is also a school of continual prayer, because, in the celebration of the "Opus Dei," the request of the disciples is renewed and at the same time answered: "Lord, teach us to pray" (Lk 11:1). The strength and the joy of your daily journey with Christ is derived, in your monasteries, from the communal celebration of the Liturgy of the Hours and of the Eucharist. The primacy and the daily obligation of these celebrations should seem to you to be the heritage of Saint Benedict, faithfully preserved and

protected from any challenge or experimentation. In this way, your life will become more and more a genuine seeking after God the Father (cf. *Rule,* 58, 7) and a participation in the Passover of the Lord, which he himself celebrates with you.

315.   You have therefore gathered in Congress in order to search for the best means of making of your houses places of Christian community, fortresses, so to speak, of prayer, and also houses of study, according to your Rule and your statutes. Your monasteries are "little monastic churches," according to the famous expression of your father, Saint Benedict: "Let the monks anticipate one another in showing consideration; let them know how to support with the greatest patience their physical and moral infirmities; let them practice obedience with emulation; let no one seek his personal advantage, but the advantage of the others; let them practice fraternal charity with a pure heart" (*Rule,* 72, 4-8). Christ is present among you if you live these virtues and walk this path; and if you know how to practice these virtues among yourselves, you will show the entire Church, and also those who seek Christ, who he is and what the name "Christian" means. Owing to these treasures placed along your path and these riches of the spiritual life, you yourselves will be capable of telling men and women who you are, why you follow Christ, how they themselves, in their own states of life, can also encounter the Lord Jesus today.

316.   As Saint Benedict also teaches, the monk knows of nothing more worthy of love than Christ (*Rule,* 5, 2), this Christ whom the monk seeks, as his worker (*Rule,* Prol. 14); the monk, in his turn, thanks to the love of Christ, travels the royal way of obedience and humility, of silence and of service, of suffering and of joy. One can thus rightly consider all this as a response to that fundamental question: who do you think, and who do you say that Christ is, you, Benedictine monks, abbots of monasteries, participants in this Congress? Here a very clear perspective for the future opens up, here also opens up an immense field

of Benedictine apostolate. Here is the portion which is yours: to know, in your midst and within you, the Lord Jesus and the wealth of his mystery, then to offer a constructive teaching to those who present themselves in your houses, your churches, your schools. I rejoice with you because of this theme of your Congress, so well-chosen. I rejoice with you because of your Benedictine tradition and the great vigor of the Benedictine life in the entire Church.

317.   I ask God to make your dialogues and deliberations of these days fruitful. I would also like to be informed of the final conclusions of the Congress and of your propositions, in order to study them. In the meantime, I express all my brotherly affection to the Very Reverend Father Abbot Primate and to each one of you. I will be spiritually present among you in the days to come, praying and wishing for the success of your labors and the future prosperity of the Benedictine family and of its undertakings.

Reflect on these very simple words. Receive also my blessing and my cordial greetings, pledge of divine protection and sign of my benevolence toward all of you.

36

TO CAPUCHIN NOVICE MASTERS, IN ROME

September 28, 1984

318.   It is with deep joy that I meet with you shortly before the feast of your Seraphic Father, Saint Francis
of Assisi, a joy which comes to my heart also because I see
the commitment with which you are implementing the
Church's recommendations on permanent formation.

At the beginning of last March, I met your provincial ministers of the Italian Conference, and now I am meeting with you who have the delicate task of forming those
who want to give themselves to God according to the
charism of Saint Francis of Assisi.

When speaking of the so-called "masters" there
spontaneously come to mind Jesus' words to the two disciples of John the Baptist who were following him and who
asked him: "'Rabbi (which means Teacher), where do you
stay?' 'Come and see,' he answered" (Jn 1:38-39).

It is one of the occasions when we see that Jesus proposes himself as a reference point by his actions. The author
of Acts will say: "...I dealt with all that Jesus did and
taught" (Acts 1:1).

No one, as the Gospel says, must be called "teacher"
(cf. Mt 23:8), or if he is, he can only do so to the degree that
he imitates the Lord Jesus.

319.   As formers of young novices, the first gift which you
must offer them is *the gift of faith.*

One cannot conceive of a religious life which is not
strongly rooted in faith and which does not grow on faith.

I therefore exhort you to educate the young men to
look into themselves and their choices with a spirit of faith.

Therefore, beloved, inspire the young men entrusted
to you to *a life of true faith!*

320. Educate them also *to hope*. The world hungers for
hope! Young people who give themselves to the sad-
dest and emptiest diversions do so because they often do
not know what it means to hope. You well know that religious life calls one to leave everything in the present for
a future reality, to leave the visible for the invisible, the
material for the spiritual.

Hope is sustained by faith and, in its turn, nourishes
faith. And both of them must be lived *in charity*.

321. Sometimes we can forget this, but Jesus' Word is
firm and clear and breaks down all resistance: it is
his commandment, the new commandment (Jn 13:34). A
Christian life, much less a religious life, cannot be conceived
which is not immersed in charity. Certainly, you must be
the first to set the example: but you also have the responsibility of verifying it in your young men.

While the contemporary world is troubled in an environment often dominated by egoism, hatred and violence,
you must be a glowing sign, a living witness of charity.

And how could a son of Francis continue to be this
sign, if he does not have charity? If, like his Seraphic
Father, he does not feel, does not love, does not live charity?

322. This is especially true for you who base your life on
brotherhood and recognize in it an essential element
of your charism. So much so, that your Constitution exhorts
you constantly to accept one another in a grateful spirit
as a gift from God (*Capuchin Constitution,* no. 84, 1) and,
according to Saint Francis' teaching and your tradition,
even wants you to consider everyone equal and "to call one
another, without distinction, brother" (*ibid.,* no. 84, 3).

323. This life of charity leads spontaneously to the life
of prayer which—as I said to your brothers, the
Italian provincial ministers—constitutes the fundamental
objective of permanent formation, because it is the pillar
of your life: "If the path of these recent years has brought
you to an apostolic activity which is perhaps too intense
and diffusive, it is time to review your choices in this regard;

give God more time and heart and mind; by your life teach the brothers that God has sacrosanct rights over man's existence and cannot be relegated to the last place in the house, to the last moment of the day. The search for intimacy with him must be the tireless commitment of your days.[1]

Especially during the period of novitiate, young men, together with you, must be committed to finding that God who manifests himself to those who seek him with a sincere heart (cf. *Capuchin Constitution*, no. 29). And you must educate them to this, above all with your life, your daily conduct, your passionate love for God's house.

324.   As Franciscan Capuchins, you must not only live austerity, *poverty of life*, but also make it shine forth. The consumerism which torments the world today and which is the cause of so many of its ills must find a kind of "dike" in you. Your Constitution affirms: "The spirit of penance in an austere life is the characteristic of our Order: following the example of Christ and Saint Francis, we choose a rigorous life" (no. 101, 5).

Form young men to authentic poverty! Young people, especially those of today, are generous, ready to give, to give themselves!

May the Mother of Jesus and our Mother, who lived in silence and in prayer along with her Son, accompany you in this so delicate and so difficult, but also so praiseworthy a work. As a sign of my affection and as a pledge of divine grace, I impart to you my heartfelt Apostolic Blessing.

---

[1] Cf. Book III—no. 185.

37

TO THE PASSIONISTS IN ROME

October 1, 1984

325.   I want to express to you my deep joy at being able to meet with you today: you who have come from every part of the world on the occasion of yesterday's beatification of your confrere, Isidore De Loor. We have all rejoiced, thanking the Lord who has been pleased to give us a new model of sanctity in the one, who, for your Congregation, is the first coadjutor brother to be raised to the altars.

Our meeting assumes a special significance, also, in view of this very important fact: that precisely this year, formal approval was given to your new Constitutions, which are intended to indicate to you how to live the Rule of Saint Paul of the Cross in the present historical situation, and according to the directives of the recent Council and the new Code of Canon Law.

My affectionate greeting is also extended to all the members of your praiseworthy and distinguished Congregation, with special regard to those who, in body and spirit, are more especially feeling the weight of the cross. To them, I want to express in a special way my encouragement and my gratitude and that of the Church itself for the contribution, mysterious but real, which they are making to the development and spread of the Kingdom of God and to the salvation of the world.

326.   Yesterday we celebrated the figure of Blessed Isidore, but I feel the need to do so again here, even if only briefly. The example that the new Blessed gives us is of such a universal nature that it proves to be highly useful not only for the coadjutor brothers of your religious family and others, but also for all the members of the People of God, whose essential values his example touches in one way or

another: family affections, friendship, social and community life, work, recreation, respect for nature, worship of the Lord. Into all these fundamental dimensions of not only Christian but also human life, Blessed Isidore was able to bring *the light and wisdom of the cross,* with which, without attitudes of exhibitionism but with great simplicity, equilibrium and naturalness, as a true Christian and religious, he was able to transform everything, raise up everything, give everything a redemptive value in Christ and with Christ.

And is this not, substantially, what each of us should and must achieve, whatever our vocation or state of life?

All things considered, the universal Christian example of Blessed Isidore amounts to this basic realization, which in a certain way summarizes the entire message of Christian wisdom: one must make of the cross the "salt of the earth": that which truly "gives flavor" to this life and directs its trials and tribulations toward the final goal of heaven.

327. The world needs true wisdom. It often seeks wisdom where it is not, and is unable to recognize it where it is truly found. And why is this so? The reason may be the one that Saint Paul underlines in the First Letter to the Corinthians (Ch. 1-2): true knowledge, which is that of the cross, sometimes appears under the aspect of "absurdity" or "folly." But—as the Apostle then explains—"the message of the cross is complete absurdity for those who are headed for ruin" (1 Cor 1:18), for those, that is, who, blinded by pride, think they are wise while in reality, in God's eyes, they are really foolish. True wisdom, then—that of the cross—is evident only to the humble and to those who seek truth, rejecting the empty facsimiles of it. Here lies the courageous and consistent teaching of Blessed Isidore. His "wisdom" was not the fruit of deep studies or of sought-after academic titles, but it was not for this reason less decisive; it was indeed a gift of the Holy Spirit for which he knew how to prepare himself by a severe asceticism, in perfect observance of the rules and of the discipline of his Congregation.

Blessed Isidore is a brother who was able to understand deeply the value and the fruitfulness of the cross, thus putting into practice the ideal of your Congregation in an eminent manner. He was able to see in the cross the source of all consolation, the inspiration for the most noble undertakings of justice, of charity and of mercy; he was able to live the mystery of the cross as the royal road to salvation and sanctity.

328.   Beloved brothers, I see present with you in spirit today the more than three thousand Passionists spread throughout the world to preach and live the message of God's infinite love, manifested in a special way in the Passion of his only Son. To you and to them goes my sincere gratitude, and that of the Church, for the good which your Congregation has achieved during these two and a half centuries of life; for the gifts of grace and of sanctity, attested by so many of its members, and in a special way by Saint Paul of the Cross, your father and your guide; by Saint Vincent Mary Strambi, bishop, shining example for the pastors of the People of God; by Blessed Dominic of the Mother of God, tireless precursor and apostle of ecumenism in the last century; and today, we joyfully add, by Blessed Isidore De Loor.

329.   Contemplating these figures who do honor to your Institute, I cannot but conclude with a sincere wish, which I have taken from a letter addressed by your Founder to his confreres in 1751: "May this small Congregation, a work of divine mercy, develop throughout the world so that...everywhere there may be holy workers who, like loud trumpets animated by the Holy Spirit, may awaken souls asleep in sin through the holy preaching of the Most Holy Sufferings of the Son of God, Christ Jesus, so that, contrite, they may shed salutary tears of repentance and with constant devout meditation on the same Most Holy Sufferings they may become ever more inflamed with the holy love of God, living devoutly according to their proper state" (*Letter* IV, 229).

I entrust these wishes to the motherly heart of Our Lady of Sorrows, Queen of your Congregation, and I commend to her each and every one of you, dear Passionists. May my Apostolic Blessing accompany you, now and always.

38

TO THE CARTHUSIANS AT
SERRA SAN BRUNO (ITALY)

October 5, 1984

330.   I heartily thank Father Prior for the warm words
of greeting he has addressed to me in the name of
the community, in this meeting that is so significant for
me, and I am sure also for you. I have very gladly come
among you to show you the affection and esteem I have for
your Order and to recall, besides, on the ninth centenary
of its foundation, the close bonds that it has woven with
the Apostolic See from its very beginning, when several
missions were entrusted to Saint Bruno and his first disciples by my venerated predecessor Urban II.

For the jubilee day I sent Father Andre Poisson, the
Minister General of the Order, a letter in which, recalling
the charism of your well-deserving institution, I noted that,
even in due and proper adaptation to the times, "always
going back to the original spirit of your Order, you must
remain in your holy resolution with unshaken will." Now
that Providence has granted this visit, I would like to take
up again the discourse begun in that letter, meditating with
you on the role that you have in the Church and on the expectations that the People of God have of you.

331.   To you it has been given to live the contemplative
vocation in this oasis of peace and prayer, which
Saint Bruno, writing to his friend Radolfo le Verd, once
described as follows: "I live in a desert place within the con-
fines of Calabria, sufficiently far removed on all sides from
the haunts of man. How can I worthily describe how
pleasant the place is, and the temperate and wholesome
climate, or the ample and pleasing plains stretching far out
between the mountains, where there are verdant fields and

217

flowering meadows? Or how can I sufficiently describe the perspective of hills rising gently on all sides, the seclusion of the dark valleys with the delightful abundance of rivers, streams, and springs?" (Saint Bruno, *Ep. ad Radulphum*, Lettres des premiers Chartreux, Sources chretiennes, Paris, 1962, p. 68). It is necessary for you, today's disciples of that great man of God, to follow his examples, committing yourselves to practicing his spirit of love for God in solitude, in silence, in prayer, like "men awaiting their master's return, so that when he arrives and knocks, they will open for him without delay" (Lk 12:36). You, in fact, have been called to live as though by anticipation that divine life which Saint Paul describes in his First Letter to the Corinthians when he observes: "Now we see indistinctly, as in a mirror; then we shall see face to face. My knowledge is imperfect now; then I shall know even as I am known" (13:12).

332. Your Founder calls upon you to reflect on the profound meaning of the contemplative life, to which God calls generous souls in every era of history. The Carthusian spirit is for strong men: Saint Bruno once noted that the contemplative commitment would be reserved to a few ("Those who devote themselves to contemplation are indeed fewer than those who devote themselves to action," Saint Bruno, *ibid.*, pp. 70, 72). But these few are called to form a sort of "avant-garde" in the Church. Work upon one's character, openness to divine grace, assiduous prayer, all this serves to forge in the Carthusian a new spirit, tempered in solitude in order to live for God in an attitude of total availability. The Carthusian is committed to completely overcoming himself and cultivating seeds of every virtue, feeding abundantly on heavenly food. In all of this there is a program for the interior life, to which Saint Bruno alludes when he writes, "Here one seeks that eye by whose serene glance the spouse is wounded by love, and in its purity and cleanness beholds God. Here is celebrated that busy leisure, and one pauses in quiet action" (*ibid.*, p. 70).

333.   The contemplative man is constantly tending toward God and can truly say with the psalmist: "When shall I go and behold the face of God?" (Ps 41:3). He sees the world and its situations much differently from one who is living in it: "quiet" is sought only in God, and Saint Bruno time and again calls upon his disciples to flee "the troubles and misfortunes" of this world and to move "from the tempest of this world into the safe and quiet haven of the port" (Saint Bruno, *ibid.,* p. 74). In the peace and silence of the monastery is found the joy of praising God, of living in him, by him and through him. Saint Bruno, who lived in this monastery for about ten years, writing to his brothers in the community of the Chartreuse, opens his soul, overflowing with joy, and without any rhetoric urges them to enjoy their contemplative state: "Rejoice, my beloved brothers," he writes, "on account of your blessed fortune and for the abundant share of God's grace in you. Rejoice because you have avoided the many dangers and shipwrecks of the fluctuating world. Rejoice because you have reached the quiet and safe haven of the more secluded port" (*ibid.,* p. 82).

334.   However, this specific and heroic vocation of yours does not put you on the margin of the Church. Rather, it places you in its very heart. Your presence is a constant call to prayer, which is the premise of every authentic apostolate. As I wrote to you, "the sacrifice of praise. . .demands your pious resourcefulness, you who stand daily 'on the divine watch' (cf. Saint Bruno)." The Church holds you in esteem, counts a great deal on your witness, and relies on your prayers. I too entrust to you my apostolic ministry as pastor of the universal Church. With your life, give witness to your love for God. The world is watching you and, perhaps unknowingly, expects a great deal from your contemplative life. Continue to put before its eyes the "provocation" of a way of life which, though imbued with suffering, solitude and silence, makes the fountain of an ever renewed joy spring forth from you. Did not your Founder write: "What divine usefulness and happiness are conferred by the solitude and silence of the desert on those who love

them are known only to those who have experienced them" (*ibid.*, p. 70)? That this is also your experience can be seen from the enthusiasm with which you persevere on the way you have undertaken. From your faces one can see how God gives the peace and joy of the Spirit as a reward to whoever has left everything to live by him and to sing his praises for ever.

335.   The Church is convinced of the current relevance of your charism, and I hope that many generous souls will follow you into the contemplative life. Yours is an evangelical way of following Christ. It demands total surrender in seclusion from the world, as a result of a courageous choice that has at its origin the sole call of Jesus. It is he who has offered you this invitation of friendship and love to follow him onto the mountain in order to remain with him.

My hope is that from this place a message may go out to the world and reach especially the young people, opening before their eyes the perspective of the contemplative life as a gift from God. Young people today are animated by great ideals and if they see consistent men, witnesses of the Gospel, they will follow them. To propose to today's world the living of a "life hidden with Christ" (Col 3:3) means to reaffirm the value of humility, poverty and interior freedom. The world, which down deep is thirsty for these virtues, wants to see upright men practicing them daily with heroism, conscious that they are loving and serving their brethren through this witness.

336.   You in this monastery are called to be the lamps that light the way on which so many brothers and sisters scattered throughout the world are walking. Always know how to help those who need your prayer and serenity. Even in the happy situation of having chosen with Mary, the sister of Martha, "the better portion...which shall not be taken away" (Lk 10:42), you are not removed from the condition of your brethren, who are knocking at the place of your solitude. They bring you their problems, their sufferings, their difficulties that accompany this life: you—while

respecting the demands of your contemplative life—give them the joy of God, assuring them that you will pray for them, that you will offer your mortifications so that they too may draw strength and courage from the fountain of life, who is Christ. They offer you the restlessness of humanity; you have them discover that God is the source of true peace. In fact, to use yet another of Saint Bruno's expressions, "What else is as good as God? Moreover, what else is good, except God alone?" (Saint Bruno, *ibid.,* p.78).

337.   I wanted to read with you some of your Founder's thoughts in order to relive in this place the witness of his intense hermitic life, the spirit that animated him. Here, after long service to the Church, he wanted to end his earthly life. Here you remain to keep the lamp burning that he lighted nine centuries ago.

I carry with me, on this pastoral visit to Calabria, the experience of a moment of peace and joy that has given me great comfort. Nature, the silence, your prayer, remain inscribed in my heart: carry on your mission. In support of your commitment, I impart to each one my Apostolic Blessing, imploring the gifts that come from God, the source of all consolation.

39

TO MEN AND WOMEN RELIGIOUS
AT THE SANCTUARY OF SAINT FRANCIS
OF PAOLA (ITALY)

October 5, 1984

338.   "Father, Lord of heaven and earth, to you I offer
       praise; for what you have hidden from the learned
and the clever you have revealed to the merest children"
(Mt 11:25). These words of Christ come spontaneously to
mind as we celebrate the Eucharist in the sanctuary which
the piety of the faithful erected in honor of a man like
Francis of Paola, who lived far from books but close to God:
he was truly one of those "merest children" whom God in-
troduces to the knowledge of his "hidden things." Francis
of Paola was certainly not a learned man, but nevertheless
he knew perfectly well the wisdom of the saints and was
better able to penetrate into hearts than those learned theologians who often turned to him for clarification of their
doubts and their bewilderment. He, a "mere child," rather
"least," as he liked to describe himself and his sons,
deserved to be the teacher of the "great" ones of the earth,
and this was thanks to the light which God poured into his
soul, which was thirsty for him.

339.   In thanking the Superior General of the Minims and
       the President of the Major Superiors of Calabria for
the words addressed to me at the beginning of the Holy
Mass, I greet this monastic community and all of you, beloved religious and consecrated souls here present. It is significant that our meeting is taking place in this sanctuary,
in which everything speaks to us of a man who was able
to give himself unreservedly to God, finding in this unconditional consecration of self the ever flowing source of an
unending charity toward his brethren. In the witness of

Francis of Paola, a figure in whom is summed up the best traits of the generous people of Calabria, there are clearly reproposed the essential elements of every life consecrated to serving God and the Church. For this reason, beloved, I am happy to meet with you in this place to tell you how much I appreciate your mission and your manifold apostolate.

340.   Calabria has always been rich in monastic and religious foundations, and has given to the Church figures of saints such as Saint Saba, Saint Nilus, Saint Bruno and Saint Francis himself. The first monasticism arrived in this region from the Near East, and here achieved a happy synthesis of spirituality and monastic-religious culture.

However, this is not just past history. The freshness of religious life is alive today in you, present and working in the ecclesial and social fabric. You, souls consecrated to God in present history, are nourished by the spirit and charism of your origins in order to give, by your witness of evangelical consistency, a convincing answer to the expectations of the present generation.

341.   Have you ever asked yourselves what the Church of Calabria and the good people of this region expect from you? In the light of the lives and teachings of your great saints, in particular of the patron of this Church, I believe that today the witness of a renewed commitment to prayer and union with God is fundamental to your credibility. The great ascetics and Founders teach that it is necessary to give God the first place in one's life and in one's apostolate in order to reach out to meet the needs of the world, which is searching breathlessly for the values which will snatch it from the anxiety and uncertainty of daily living. You will provide a reference point for the many brothers and sisters lost along the roads of the world if you are able to be joyful witnesses of the Gospel in all its fullness.

342. Thirst for God is widespread: it is up to the members of religious Institutes to channel this need, reviving in their daily witness the joy of living with God and by God, this God who does not alienate the spirit and does not take away freedom, but who enriches the soul and makes it free to savor his presence. Is this not the experience that you have when, with complete availability, you are able to follow Christ, chaste, poor and obedient to the Father? Do you not find in this the secret of true peace of soul? Share this style of life with your brothers and sisters, strongly emphasizing the joy of being together, "of one heart and one mind" in the generous sharing of all your goods (cf. Acts 4:32). Do not be afraid of feeling misunderstood: Christ is with you to instill hope and strength in you, that you may carry it enthusiastically to your brothers and sisters. The world can well distinguish your evangelical witness from any other: not for nothing does it set its ideology and its fleeting values against you.

343. Today, living in union with God, insisting on the spirit of prayer, is an obligatory path for religious life: the Church needs consecrated souls who live in the interiority of their relationship with God and affirm God's primacy before the world, that the world may understand that it is not material goods, success or pleasures which give man serenity, but the degree of union with Christ, man's true hope.

344. Consecration to God, which allows you to "follow Christ more freely and imitate him more nearly" (*Perfectae Caritatis,* 1), does not cut you off from the problems of your brothers and sisters: the characteristic of the religious life of this land—where many towns and villages owe their origin to the presence of a convent or monastery, even inheriting from it their name—calls upon you to combine the spirit of union with God with solidarity toward the brethren, who expect a great deal from your indefatigable commitment to the apostolate. The economic hardships inherited from the past and which are still far from a rightful solution, and the evils of today's society, from which

young people especially suffer, appear before your eyes every day. You cannot ignore them by taking refuge in your communities. You too must bear their burden, from your own angle, obviously with respect for the charism proper to your respective Institutes. For that matter, there is no true religious life, rooted in intimate union with Christ, which is not carried over into the need to follow him and to serve him in his members (cf. *Perfectae Caritatis,* 8).

Your witness must not be separated from awareness of the situations of the people surrounding you, who rely on your spiritual and concrete help, who expect your act of brotherly love, who see in each one of you the brother who can understand them and, in the name of Christ, save them.

345.   Nevertheless, those who approach you do not always do so to ask for something: often the Lord has you meet a brother as a reminder, a reflection, an incentive to a more authentic evangelical witness. May you be able to welcome as providential these calls to take up religious life again with more courage and evangelical spirit.

To be poor among the poor is a gift from the Lord: in touch with concrete situations, the Word of the Lord becomes more incisive and calls upon us to read the parable of the man who fell among robbers (Lk 10:25-37) with a greater sense of personal participation. Your founding saints gave rise to apostolic communities which, combining asceticism and charity, directed their mission towards those categories of persons whom society often casts aside, but whom the Church considers treasures for the Kingdom. How can we not recall in this place the continuous flow of faithful who came from the city and nearby hamlets to meet the hermit Francis? A man of God and a tireless worker, he received them kindly, listened to them willingly, clarified their doubts, at times even solved their problems with a miracle, and, when seeing them off, always left in them that "satisfaction and peace"—sources say—which is worth much more than material goods and health itself. These regions were witnesses then of the wonders described by Isaiah in the passage we have just heard:

"Then will the eyes of the blind be opened,
the ears of the deaf be cleared.
Then will the lame leap like a stag,
then the tongue of the dumb will sing.
Streams will burst forth in the desert, and rivers in
the steppe" (Is 35:5-6).

346. The spiritual heritage of the religious life of this
region often sinks its roots into the social field, not
to replace the public structures, but to help them in the
difficult task of aiding and saving the neediest brethren.
Do not ignore this point of view now that the Church is
reaffirming her presence in the fields of education and
work. Those who are in need always look to your witness
and you must not betray the trust of those who have no
social voice. May you always be attentive to their cry for
help and give proof of your love for Christ by doing all you
can for the brethren. It is not words which are lacking in
this sector of society, it is action. You are called, in the name
of Christ, to supply this action with unselfish participation,
with solidarity in extreme cases, with the commitment to
involve persons of good will in helping those who are truly
in need.

347. Doing this, you will see opportunities for charity
open up before you and you will reaffirm the insup-
pressible dignity of each person, rediscovering Christ's
suffering face in the features of those who are tried by mis-
fortune. Above all, you will relive the history of your call,
which is steeped in the Lord's love and mercy. The Gospel
opens up before you every day and calls you to the apostolate: every man is a living page of it, and he must be understood and welcomed in one's own experience of faith.
Never tire of offering your hand to those who are in need:
your gesture of solidarity may be the opening through
which a brother will be able to glimpse the providence of
the Father, who looks after everyone and who gives everyone a purpose in this world. "At the same time as being
a challenge to the world and to the Church herself, your
silent witness of poverty and abnegation, of purity and

sincerity, of self-sacrifice in obedience can become an eloquent witness capable of touching also non-Christians who
have good will and are sensitive to certain values" (*Evangelii Nuntiandi,* 69, 2).

348.   This embodiment of your religious life in the eccle-
          sial and social fabric of Calabria is the message
which I give to you today in this place sanctified by the
ascetic and man of God, Saint Francis of Paola. May you
be able to draw from union with God, daily present in his
Eucharistic banquet, the strength for evangelical witness
to everyone: to the simple, the poor, the small, those discriminated against, the suffering, the learned, those who
work the soil, those from the world of work, those who are
open to dialogue and even those who exclude themselves
from it at the moment. Christ precedes you and gives you
strength, because he is the goal and the measure of your
life: from your daily dialogue with him you draw that
supernatural charity about which Saint Paul spoke to us
in that sublime passage from the First Letter to the Corinthians that we heard a short time ago: that is, a charity
which "is not self-seeking, is not prone to anger; neither
does it brood over injuries. Love does not rejoice in what
is wrong but rejoices with the truth. There is no limit
to love's forbearance, to its trust, its hope, its power
to endure" (13:5-7).

349.   Only those who are completely detached from them-
          selves can accept totally the radical demands of a
charity which, according to the words of the Apostle, "has
no limits": ". . .There is no limit. . . to its trust, its hope,
its power to endure." But who better than the religious can
achieve in himself such detachment? In being committed
to the way of the evangelical counsels, is he not moved by
the desire to bring about in himself that stripping of everything, which can more completely make room for everything of God's? May you be able to appreciate in their full
value, beloved, the vows of chastity, poverty and obedience
which you will shortly be renewing. They do not hamper
nor limit your personality, but rather free it for the possi-

bility of a more constant and more generous gift in your daily service to God and the brethren.

In the footsteps of your great saints, and in particular of the one whose spirit hovers in this church, may you be happily chaste, poor and obedient. You will experience, as they experienced, the truth of Christ's words: ". . . my yoke is easy and my burden light" (Mt 11:30), and, like them, you too will be able to share your experience with many "weary and oppressed" brethren who come to you for a word that can restore their hope.

40

TO PRIESTS, RELIGIOUS AND SEMINARIANS IN PUERTO RICO

October 12, 1984

350.   During this visit to Puerto Rico, which I have been looking forward to for some time, it gives me particular satisfaction to gather here with you, the vital force of the Church on this beautiful island which Columbus christened with the name of the Lord's precursor: Saint John the Baptist.

The Pope is very conscious of your importance for the Church, and of the self-surrender and sacrifice with which you are carrying out your pastoral mission as messengers of the Gospel, witnesses to the faith, and servants of your brothers. Hence, during this apostolic journey which marks the initial preparations for the commemorative activities celebrating the fifth centenary of the discovery and evangelization of America, I made sure that I set aside this special time—all too brief, by force of circumstances—to meet with you, who are (or will be in due course) consecrated to the Lord.

I would like to be able to greet you all personally, one by one; to learn of your apostolic activities, to know your anxieties, your problems, your joys and sorrows; to hear your confidences and hopes, and the yearnings of so many hearts full of love for Christ and the Church.

But above all, I would like this gathering to be for you an occasion which lifts your spirits—a moment of encouragement in your lives as witnesses of Christ, as apostles, as people who have devoted your lives to the service of God and your brothers. You should be fully aware that, to a large extent, the building up of the Church in Puerto Rico depends on your apostolic activity as messengers and dispensers of the blessings of salvation. Therefore, closely united to your bishops and superiors, you really have to be "the salt of the earth and light of the world" in our own day (Mt 5:13-14)—each according to his or her own station in life. A "salt," that is, which gives a new inspiration to society; and a "light" which illuminates horizons beyond those which merely human considerations can aspire to.

351.   Beloved priests—diocesan and religious: never cease to examine your own interior life in the light of a faith which is renewed every day. You are chosen ones, friends of Jesus, servants of his plan of salvation. Stewards of the mysteries of God on behalf of your communities, enriched with powers higher than your own personal gifts by virtue of the endowment you received by the imposition of hands (cf. 2 Tim 1:6), you are the arms, the voice, and the heart of Christ, who continues saving men and women today through the mediation of your ministry in the Church.

Hence, you must revive in your hearts the yearnings, hopes and graces which you received through your priestly ordination. Remember how often you act "in the person of Christ," and "in the power of the Holy Spirit." You have an interior dynamism transcending human capacities which must carry you forward—with humility, but with great confidence—toward your own inner plenitude, which constitutes maturity of life in Christ: "The Spirit God has given us is no cowardly spirit, but rather one that makes us strong, loving, and wise. Therefore, never be ashamed of your testimony to our Lord" (2 Tim 1:7-8).

352.   Yes, my dear brothers in the priesthood: looking towards Christ as your model, and as the power which can rejuvenate your spirits day by day, rejoice in your own special identity as priests! Never succumb to doubts in regard to the value of your priestly life, or the possibility of persevering faithfully in it. Never are you left alone with nothing more than your own human resources: "God is our refuge and our strength, an ever-present help in distress. Therefore we fear not..." (Ps 46 [45]:2ff.).

But at the same time, be mindful of your frailty. To overcome it, a constant and resolute union with Christ in

230

prayer is absolutely essential. You need the grace of the sacraments, which are also for you the source of renewal and grace. Nourished by Christ himself—that inexhaustible fountain, faithful to your daily meditation as well as to the recitation of the Liturgy of the Hours, and with a deep filial love for the Mother of Jesus, who is the Mother of us all, you will be able to maintain undiminished the vigor and freshness of your commitment.

353.   The souls entrusted to your care expect a great deal from you. Do not withhold from them a generous gift of self: "The gift you have received, give as a gift"(Mt 10:8).

The love for Christ must be effective in inspiring love for your fellowman, especially for those who are most in need. But, in the first place, everyone should be able to recognize you as teachers and friends in the faith, followers of Christ, builders of the Church, preachers of brotherhood and dialogue, who give themselves generously in working for the progress and advancement of man.

In the exercise of your ministry, always remain united to your bishops, who are the centers of the Church's life at the diocesan level. That unity which springs from the very nucleus of our Christian faith, and pertains to the essential core of the Church, becomes more necessary than ever in times of difficulty. Never yield, therefore, to the temptation to ignore or act against the directives of your pastors. Any apparent advances in pastoral effectiveness which might seem to justify such disobedience will be spurious.

In the course of your ministry you will sometimes be faced with issues which involve specific choices of a political nature. In such situations you must be constant in proclaiming the moral principles which govern every field of human activity. But lay people with morally upright consciences are those best qualified for the ordering of temporal matters according to God's plan. Leave such matters to them. Your task is to foster communion and brotherhood; not to provoke discord in regard to matters where the faithful may legitimately choose between different courses of action. In drawing this matter to the attention of priests, both diocesan and religious, I would add that these remarks are equally applicable to the other members of religious families.

354. What can be said now of a more specific nature to you, the religious brothers and sisters of Puerto Rico? Recalling the words of the Apocalypse, I would like to reaffirm with joy: "I know your deeds—your love and faith and service—as well as your patient endurance" (Rev 2:19). I am aware of your capable presence in various fields of the Church's apostolate: in parishes, with children, with students, the sick and needy, the poor and outcast, the well-educated, and with so many others who confidently approach you seeking advice and encouragement. I rejoice in this whole presence in the Church that you represent by your work and your love for man, for the sake of Christ. In this connection, allow me to remind you that, as souls consecrated to God, your first duty is to be *specialists in the Gospel of Jesus*—men and women who are committed to that perfect love of God and neighbor which sums up the essence of the Gospel.

It is in this *dynamism of holiness*, following the particular charism of each Institute, that the religious vocation finds its true meaning and fulfillment. It is a fundamental attitude of service: a "school of service to the Lord," to use the beautiful phrase found in the Rule of Saint Benedict (*Rule*, pr. 45).

355. Always keep firmly in mind that just as it is the lay vocation to provide a Christian witness in the temporal sphere, the consecrated soul must bear witness to Christ by a life which travels *the path of the Beatitudes.* Such a life must be a joyful embodiment of the demands of chastity, poverty, and obedience, involving an active participation in the life of one's own community and constant fidelity to an intense life of prayer, since "every worthwhile gift, every genuine benefit comes from above, descending from the Father of the heavenly luminaries" (James 1:17).

Therefore, do not allow yourselves to be dazzled by the mirage of an excessive activism which can hinder your

232

intimacy with the Lord. And never yield to the easy temptation to underestimate the value of life in community, or to open the door to motivations foreign to the Gospel. If you permit these to inspire your lifestyle, your true identity as religious will become blurred.

356.   I am also aware of the presence here today of a group of young people representing the more than 300 students currently receiving formation in the major seminary, and in various religious Institutes. My heart—the heart of a pastor—is filled with the deepest joy on their behalf, since they embody the future hopes of the Church on this island. My dear young people, no long speeches are necessary in order to make clear my great affection for you, and my desire to confirm you in the path you have chosen. I exhort you to keep that flame of generosity burning brightly, and always to remain faithful to the call which God has inscribed in your hearts. Faced with the demanding but splendid task which awaits you, be aware of how important this time of preparation is. Like the faithful and prudent servant in the Gospel, develop to their utmost potential the talents you have received (cf. Mt 25:14-22), so as to place them at the disposal of the Church and of those who await your future ministry.

357.   It is encouraging for me, and a cause for giving thanks to the Father, to see priestly and religious vocations flourishing in Puerto Rico. What bright hopes this raises! It proves that the Church is sinking her roots ever more deeply within the noble souls of the Puerto Rican people. This development has now reached the truly wonderful point where all the bishops are natives of the island, and Puerto Rico has its first cardinal.

Nevertheless, this growth does not yet satisfy the need, and so there must be continuing efforts to promote vocations to the consecrated life by all possible means. This is a task which pertains to the entire Christian community.

This island, which will soon celebrate 500 years of evangelization, has received—and still receives today—the valuable and self-sacrificing assistance of other brothers and sisters in the faith who come from overseas countries. They have given themselves to the utmost on behalf of this Church, and still continue to do so. To all of them I wish to say: Thank you, in the name of Christ! Thank you for your generosity! Thank you for opening your hearts! Continue working in this Church which offers you its hospitality. It is your Church too—the Church of Christ in Latin America.

358. I conclude with a prayer to the Lord that the "National Pastoral Plan for the Occasion of the Fifth Centenary of the Evangelization of America," prepared by your bishops, may produce abundant fruits for the Church which proceeds along its pilgrim way in the land of "Borinquen"—and in the first place for you.

I entrust to your prayers the responsibilities of my own ministry as Successor of Peter, and I assure you of my prayers that the Mother of Divine Providence will help you, comfort you with her maternal care, and keep you faithful to your commitment in the Church. With these desires I impart with warm affection to you, and to all those whom you represent, my Apostolic Blessing.

41

TO THE RELIGIOUS OF THE HOSPITALLER ORDER OF SAINT JOHN OF GOD, IN ROME

December 23, 1984

359.　At the end of my visit to the "San Pietro" Hospital, managed and administrated with such care by the Brothers of Saint John of God, I am delighted for the chance to meet with you alone during this brief encounter.

I wish, first of all, to express my profound esteem for the work you perform here in this Roman hospital and in all the other works entrusted to you: in Rome, in Italy, and in other countries around the world. Your task is an arduous, delicate, generous one, and it is so necessary because, yes, the sick need treatment and medicine, but at the same time they need comprehension, moral and spiritual aid, and ideals: just as was understood and taught by your Blessed Founder, well-tested by the memorable episodes of his adventurous existence.

360.　At the same time, I wish also to urge you on towards a fervent perseverance in your commitment to caring, despite the difficulties and incomprehension which you may face, given the current political and social situation. Saint John of God, during a dramatic period (1495-1550), in the midst of difficulties which often proved terrible, continued along his way with a deep faith and a daily, intense dedication. He wrote the following in a letter: "Our fortitude tells us to be strong and content in the service of God, showing a happy face unto the world whether it be in travail, tribulation, fatigue and sickness, or prosperity and joy, and for both we must give thanks to Jesus Christ."

361.   Have faith in the Incarnation! As the Christmas festivities draw near, I am led to emphasize this fundamental part of your religious life, following the example of your Founder.

To have faith in the Incarnation means, in the first place, *to have a firm belief in Divine Providence.* God, in fact, has given a concrete demonstration of his love for humanity by joining it, both as man and Savior: "In this is love"— writes Saint John—"not that we loved God, but that he loved us and sent his Son to be the expiation for our sins" (1 John 4: 10). Many of the events of recent history shock and disturb us: "Christian anthropology" founded on the concept of the "human person" created by God, redeemed by Christ, shown the light by the Church, responsible through eternity for his own acts, stands in contrast to immanentistic and historicistic anthropology, which have no ties to Revelation. You, also, who live in direct contact with so many human problems and individual cases, must realize as much and experience pain and suffering. And yet the celebration of Christmas returns, continuing to underline the fact that "the Word was made flesh," in order to enlighten humanity both as to its true destiny and to the presence of divine love in the trials and tribulations of history. One needs the humility of your Holy Founder to accept and live this truth.

362.   Having faith in the Incarnation, then, means *loving man,* whoever he may be, *as God's creation.* The very fact that God wanted to make himself "man" clearly shows how much he loved, respected, and valued mankind. This spirituality always accompanied Saint John of God, leading him to live a life of continual charity, especially towards the poorest and the neediest, while inspiring him, on occasion, to acts of great heroism. Certainly, times have changed quite a bit since then; and yet suffering has not disappeared, and, in many places, misery and neglect endure. Your spirituality could be defined as one of *"Ecce Homo,"* in the sense that you are able to see Christ in every person who suffers, and you are able to serve him with love and worship.

363.　And, finally, having faith in the Incarnation also means *leading souls to their salvation*. It was for this, in fact, that Jesus was born in the stable in Bethlehem and died on the Cross. "God, who is rich in mercy, out of the great love with which he loved us, even when we were dead through our trespasses, made us alive together with Christ; by grace you have been saved" (Eph 2:4-5). This was Saint John's intention, and it should also be your apostolic concern, delicate and discreet, and yet constant and stimulating.

364.　The Church has entrusted you with a very important task: you are apostles inside the hospitals, both in your dealings with the doctors and nurses, and in your loving care of the sick. How many of your fellow brothers have shown themselves to be well-deserving in the four hundred and more years of your Institute's history: doctors, surgeons, pharmacologists, scholars, nurses, and also theologians, apologists, scientists. Among many, I would like to recall the venerable Servant of God, Brother Benedetto Menni, who brought about the great restoration of the Order in Spain and founded the Hospitaller Sisters of the Sacred Heart of Jesus. A miracle was recently recognized which can be attributed to his intercession.

365.　In following your vocation, you have given up everything to put yourselves at the service of the sick: I wholeheartedly wish you the spiritual joy of those whose every act is inspired by love!

May our Blessed Lady inspire, comfort, and protect each and every one of you. And may the favor of my Apostolic Blessing go with you, even as I extend it, with love, to all your confreres around the world.